READING THE BIBLE TODAY

READING THE BIBLE TODAY

A 21st-Century Appreciation of Scripture

Edgar V. McKnight

Smyth & Helwys Publishing, Inc.
6316 Peake Road
Macon, Georgia 31210-3960
1-800-747-3016
©2003 by Smyth & Helwys Publishing

Library of Congress Cataloging-in-Publication Data

McKnight, Edgar V.
Reading the Bible today : a 21st century appreciation of scripture /
Edgar V. McKnight.
p. cm.
ISBN 1-57312-407-9 (alk. paper)
1. Bible—Hermeneutics.
I. Title.
BS476 .M347 2003
220.6'1—dc21

2002152658

Table of Contents

To Jim and Pat, Dick and Margaret, and Bob and Barbara

As a Southern Baptist concerned about a fundamentalist "takeover" of the Southern Baptist Convention, I was surprised and happy that fundamentalist leaders were planning to introduce a resolution at the 1984 meeting of the convention opposing the ordination of women to the ministry. I was *surprised* that fundamentalist leaders could be so foolish as to choose the issue of women's ordination as a vehicle to continue their takeover of the Southern Baptist Convention. I was *happy* because I was convinced that the majority of the messengers at the convention would not vote for such a resolution, that the messengers' devotion to the gospel message of freedom and equality would override their allegiance to the fundamentalist leaders. I was mistaken. The messengers voted for that resolution! Since that time, the fundamentalist leaders of the convention have advanced their patriarchal agenda. In 1998 an amendment to the *Baptist Faith and Message* was adopted declaring that "a wife is to submit herself graciously to the servant leadership of her husband." In 2000, the stipulation was made that "the office of pastor is limited to men as qualified by Scripture."

Those who support such actions cite a multitude of biblical passages that present a patriarchal worldview with women submitting to men. Those who oppose such a move, however, can quote verses that challenge the severe patriarchal worldview. As a collection of ancient writings, the Bible does reflect a patriarchal culture. As the contemporary word of God, the Bible opposes a patriarchal relationship between men and women. The conflict of interpretations goes beyond the issue of the role of women in the church and in society. However, this particular issue has created the need for a fresh appreciation of the nature of the Bible as the ever-contemporary word of God and the Bible as a collection of ancient writings.

To be faithful to the Bible and our contemporary culture, we must recognize that the word of God came to our spiritual ancestors in cultures different from our own. We must learn how to distinguish between the ancient culture and the good news. As a result of discerning the word of God in the words of men and women in ancient times and places, twenty-first-century readers of the Bible will be able to do more than quote passages that transcend the culture (for example, Paul's admonition that in Christ "there is no longer male and female" [Gal 3:26]). Readers will be able to distinguish between the cultural circumstances of origin of the biblical writings and the abiding message of Holy Scripture.

This volume is dedicated to introducing the Bible to a generation of Christians who remain convinced of the authority of Scripture and who want to discover how to discern God's word for today's world. The volume begins with two chapters dealing with the reality, necessity, and value of the complete human nature of the Bible: "We have this treasure in clay jars" (1 Cor 4:7). The next three chapters sketch the specific geographical and historical setting of the Bible and discuss the contribution of archaeology to our understanding of the geographical, historical, and religious context. The major theme of the Bible—the message contained in the "clay jars"— and the language and literary means of expounding the message are covered in chapters 6, 7, and 8. The formation of the canon and the translation of the Bible into English are traced in chapters 9–13. The final chapter deals with the varieties of possible, even necessary, readings of the Bible in light of its character as word of God in historical and literary form.

Chapter 1

Word of God and Human Words – A Key to Reading the Bible

The Bible belongs to the whole world as does no other book. Written originally in Hebrew and Greek more than eighteen centuries ago, it is now available, in whole or in part, in more than a thousand languages. It has been a best-seller since best-sellers were first recognized. Its contents are widely known. Biblical phrases enrich current speech: "the skin of our teeth," "the sweat of our brow," "a thorn in the flesh," and "the salt of the earth." Speakers use a rich treasure of biblical stories as a part of the common heritage.

Christians affirm that the Bible is the supreme authority for faith and practice and search its pages for God's message. They agree on a large number of teachings gained from earnest Bible study. Frequently, however, sincere Christians, even those in the same denomination and congregation, interpret this same book differently.

In the distant past, honest people differed over the shape of the earth, and some used the Bible to show that the earth was flat! Just a century ago, certain Christians used the Bible to prove that slaves should be given their freedom, while others declared that the Bible clearly teaches that it is God's will for individuals to own other human beings as property. Today, the same Bible is used to demonstrate that capital punishment is wrong and also that it is within God's plan for people to be put to death for certain crimes. The Bible is used for liberation—of the poor, of women, and of other minorities—but it is also used consciously and deliberately in ways that keep some groups and individuals in submission. Christians may well despair at times of understanding the teachings of the Bible.

Is it really possible to understand the Bible, to discern the voice of God from a study of the Scriptures? Yes! The Bible can be understood, and this volume is designed to serve as a guide to opening the Bible and learning from its riches. The history of the reading of the Bible helps to explain and to mediate, if not to do away with, the conflict in interpretation. In the earliest period of reading and interpretation of the Bible, the Bible was read as an oracle of God. Historical and literary factors were subordinated to the religious message. Assumptions about what Scripture meant and how it was to be read supported an oracular view of the Bible and a credulous approach to it. The Bible was seen as cryptic or mysterious, meaning more than what it says. The Bible was seen as a great book of instruction with immediate relevance for readers by the discernment of what it says and means. The Bible was considered perfect and perfectly harmonious. Apparent disagreements were, therefore, to be clarified by properly determining what it says and means. The Bible, then, is divinely inspired.

With the development of critical tools and approaches to the natural world and to history and literature came a critical approach to the Bible. Instead of simply coming to the Bible to discern a divine word, people approached the Bible as data to be examined by various criteria. Instead of beginning with assumptions about ultimate divine purposes and results, interpreters asked questions about human historical authors and their purposes in writing for readers in particular locations. Historical-critical approaches were developed to answer historical questions, and literary-critical approaches were developed to answer literary questions. In some measure, instead of *reducing* the Bible to oracle, the Bible was *reduced* to history or to literature. A challenge in our day is to read the Bible as word of God while acknowledging that the Bible is also the words of humans in particular historical and social locations influenced by human languages and literary conventions.

A Human-Divine Book

The answer to the question "What is the Bible?" is of great importance. The fact is that it can be read as word of God, a revelation from the Lord God. It can also be read as human literature, produced by men and women to meet human needs. These two aspects of the Bible, the human and the divine, seem opposed to one another, but this human-divine relationship is an important key to a proper understanding of the message of the Scriptures.

Through the ages, men and women have heard God speak through the Bible, and they have confessed that it is the word of God. Let us look at the record. As early as the later New Testament period, a writer declared that he and his fellow

Christians understood the voice of God in the Scriptures, "because no prophecy ever came by human will, but men and women moved by the Holy Spirit spoke from God" (2 Pet 1:21).

The established church and its tradition came to be important factors in the reading and interpretation of the Bible—so much so that in later history the significance of the Bible was obscured among some Christians, but the reformers reaffirmed the importance of the Scriptures. "The true Christian pilgrimage," Luther said, "is . . . to the prophets, the Psalms, and the Gospels." When asked to repudiate his books and ideas, Luther stated, "My conscience is captive to the Word of God. I cannot and I will not recant anything, for to go against conscience is neither right nor safe. God help me. Amen."[1]

Early Baptists in England representing a free-church tradition arrived at their convictions about God and humankind through a belief that God speaks through the Bible. They were careful to include a statement concerning the Bible in their early confessions. In 1644, seven Baptist congregations in London prepared a statement of their views:

> The rule of . . . Knowledge, Faith, and Obedience, concerning the worship and service of God, and all other Christian duties, is not mans inventions, opinions, devices, lawes, constitutions, or traditions unwritten whatsoever, but onley the word of God contained in the Canonical Scriptures. In this written Word God hath plainly revealed whatsoever he hath thougbt needfull for us to know, beleeve, and acknowledge, touching the Nature and Office of Christ, in whom all the promises are Yea, and Amen to the praise of God.[2]

The Southern Baptist Convention of 1963 adopted a statement of faith (a revision of a statement adopted in 1925, which in turn was a revision of the 1833 New Hampshire Confession):

> The Holy Bible was written by men divinely inspired and is the record of God's revelation of Himself to man. It is a perfect treasure of divine instruction. It has God for its author, salvation for its end, and truth, without any mixture of error, for its matter. It reveals the principles by which God judges us; and therefore is, and will remain to the end of the world, the true center of Christian union, and the supreme standard by which all human conduct, creeds, and religious opinions should be tried. The criterion by which the Bible is to be interpreted is Jesus Christ.[3]

This statement ties together the view of the Bible as word of God and human words when it speaks of the fact that divinely inspired human beings authored the biblical writings and that the biblical writings constitute a "record of God's revelation of Himself to man."

A revision of this statement of faith was adopted by the Southern Baptist Convention in 2000. The revision seems to alter the balance between the Bible as word of God and as human words by deleting the statement of the Bible being a record of God's self. The Bible, then, is read simply as oracle. It is thought by some that considering human historical and literary factors makes the Bible problematic as direct divine oracle. The necessity of interpretation relativizes the authority of the Bible. Instead of correlating the Bible as revelation with the Bible as historical and literary source, the Bible as revelation is correlated with authoritative creeds. In fact, the *Baptist Faith and Message* has become more of a creed than a confession.

The value of reading the Bible in light of creeds and confessions of the churches need not be denied in order to affirm also the value and necessity of reading the Bible in light of its character as historical and literary product and record. That the books of the Bible share the characteristics of all other forms of literature is obvious to the most casual reader. Biblical writings are in human language. The original Hebrew and Greek were particular human languages, not divine dialects. Human authors whose vocabularies and styles of writing varied wrote the books. Their writings were colored by human circumstance. For example, specific matters of history and geography influenced their writings.

The forms of the literature vary. There are stories, dramas, chronicles, poems of nature, poems of love and war, hymns for public and private worship, letters, sermons, biographies, essays, and other forms. The Bible cannot be read simply as a formal confession of faith, or as an official statement of doctrine. The Bible must be read as literature in a way that formal statements can never be read.

The fact of the human element in the Bible is so obvious that no statement of it should be necessary. But it is easy to assume that, because the Bible is "a perfect treasure of divine instruction," it cannot partake of human characteristics. The writer of 2 Peter did not assume this. He declared emphatically that the Scriptures were not merely human in origin. Individuals and groups of believers did not simply decide to write the Scriptures. God is the origin, but human beings were actually involved in the process.

Importance of Human and Divine in Interpretation

Sometimes students of the Bible have emphasized one aspect of the Bible to the exclusion of the other. It is possible to read the Bible simply as an oracle from God and to ignore its human characteristics. Many of the psalms, the teachings of Jesus, and sections of the letters of Paul (to mention only a portion) can be read in this way. An understanding of the physical, historical, and social surroundings is not necessary for an appreciation of the message. Knowledge of the different literary forms and the conventions followed by ancient writers is not vital.

This kind of oracular and credulous reading is profitable for many sections of the Bible. But what does a Christian do with the less oracular and less "inspiring" sections that remain a part of God's word? One way, of course, is to treat these sections as the vehicle for symbolic meanings—to read them as oracles, as cryptic and mysterious writings with special messages for those who are able to decipher the writings.

Reacting to reading the Scriptures solely as an oracle, some people may emphasize the human aspect of the Bible to such an extent that its teachings become merely the opinions of human beings. If carried to a logical conclusion, this means that, instead of interpreting the Bible, readers and interpreters disregard its religious teachings as authoritative and approach the Bible as they would any other literature.

To ignore either aspect of the Scriptures is dangerous. Both the divine and the human must be kept in mind in order to perceive the voice and learn the will of God. Therefore, the matter is not one of deciding which words are human and which contain a divine message. They are all human. They grow out of specific physical, historical, and social environments. They are subject to all of the characteristics of other literature. But, more importantly, they are a means of revealing God and of helping men and women to know God's reality and will.

Christians are not dependent upon some highly subjective, mystical experience in which they perceive the will of God. Nor are they dependent upon some other human who supposedly has higher spiritual insight. Because the Bible is written in the "language" of men and women, they can read the Scriptures and know God who has revealed God's self among God's people and, for Christians, supremely in Jesus Christ.

Individuals who can read letters, newspapers, novels, biographies, histories, and other forms of literature can read and understand the Bible. If they accept that fact, they are already on the road toward an understanding of the Scriptures. A letter from a friend is best understood when certain facts that help make sense of the letter are known. People appreciate history when they know something of the general background against which the events are depicted and the general geographical features of the area being discussed. Readers enjoy novels and poetry more when they are aware of the literary forms and figures used.

If such matters as geography, history, language, and forms are important for an understanding of other literature, they are vital for an understanding of the Bible.

This volume discusses these matters and shows how they are related to understanding the Scriptures. It also shows how different sorts of readings enrich understanding of the Bible today.

Notes

[1] Roland H. Bainton, *Here I Stand: A Life of Martin Luther* (New York: Abingdon Press, 1956), 367, 185.

[2] Articles VII and VIII of "A Confession of Faith of Seven Congregations of Churches of Christ in London, which are commonly (but unjustly) called anabaptists," quoted in W. J. McGlothlin, *Baptist Confessions of Faith* (Philadelphia: American Baptist Publication Society, 1911), 176.

[3] *Annual of the Southern Baptist Convention*, 1963, 270.

Chapter 2

Errantry and Inerrancy

An emphasis on the *literal* accuracy of the Bible and a frequent use of the word "inerrant" are characteristic of many who want to affirm the authority of the Bible. "The Bible is either totally without any sort of error or it has no authority," they claim. I disagree. I argue that our contemporary understanding of "inerrancy" must be constrained by an understanding of the "errantry" of the Bible. Certain static views of inerrancy call into question the dynamic errantry of the Bible. By errantry, I mean the sort of activity associated with the knight-errant. (The words "errant" and "errantry" come from a root meaning "to rove," "to wander.") The knight-errant was distinguished from the knight who lived in the household of his lord and whose equipment and maintenance were cared for by this master. The lord used these "kept" knights as personal bodyguards or as soldiers in wars with rival lords. The knight-errant, in contrast to the "kept" knight, went out into the world with no other possessions than his horse, armor, and weapons and with no resources other than his skill and courage.

The errantry of the Bible is akin to what John Robinson referred to when he declared to the pilgrim fathers before they left for America:

> I cannot sufficiently bewail the condition of the Reformed Churches who are come to a Period in Religion and will go at present no further than the instruments of their Reformation. The Lutheran can't be drawn to go beyond what Luther saw; whatever part of His will our God has revealed to Calvin, they will rather die than embrace it; and the Calvinists, you see, stick fast where they were left by that great man of God, who yet saw not all things. . . . I beseech you remember, it is an article of your church

covenant, that you be ready to receive whatever truth shall be made known to you from the written Word of God.[1]

Robinson viewed the Bible as the knight-errant, not as the "kept" knight refusing to venture into the unknown future.

Demands and Problems of the Ancient Form of Inerrancy

The idea of inerrancy grows out of the idea of the Bible as Word of God. As Word of God, the Bible must be true in terms of absolute correspondence to objective reality. This is easy to accept in an abstract and deductive fashion: Bible = Word of God = absolute truth. But does the simple formula work in practice? As the ancient form of the idea of inerrancy, abstract and deductive, has been applied to the Bible in the modern scientific world, an exact correspondence between isolated statements of the Bible—even incidental ones—and objective reality has been demanded. Incidental statements and indirect allusions to the natural world, for example, must be made to correspond to the reality of the natural world, not simply to what the ancients thought of nature. Believers are seen as faulting the Bible when they acknowledge that biblical statements—on scientific matters, for example—are informed and constrained by particular ancient cultures and understandings that differ from their own. One way we can avoid faulting the Bible (in an attempt to maintain this static view of inerrancy) is to reproduce the ancient culture of the Bible in our own thinking, in our churches, in our total culture. Then we can be confident of complete one-to-one correspondence without complications.

However, a complete return to the ancient culture of the biblical world is impossible. Thus, when confronted with particular anomalies in actual experience, we "massage" the doctrine of inerrancy and the biblical data so that, on the one hand, the doctrine does not seem to be damaged and, on the other hand, we are able to live as contemporary men and women in our contemporary culture. One way that static inerrantists avoid the conflict between theory and practice is to admit that the Bible *in use* contains information not precisely in conformity with whatever standards of perfection they are using, but that some original form of the Bible (no longer available) was as perfect as God is perfect. By hook or crook, we have even accommodated the actual available Bible to the modern world when it was inevitable. In doing this, however, we move away from a static inerrancy. In respect to slavery, for example, we saw that the biblical picture of the God of Jesus Christ illuminating the pilgrimage of God's people was not consistent with the occasional biblical statements supporting and allowing slavery—statements that reflect an ancient culture. Mature theological insights properly called into question the inadequate social assumptions supported by ancient culture. The Bible, and not simply human opinions and judgments, made clear the partial understandings and incomplete ethical injunctions of sections of the Bible itself. In spite of current problems of accommodation, the same thing is happening with inadequate views of the relationship of men and women. The insight that in Christ "there is no longer male and female" (Gal 3:28) challenges inadequate social assumptions and their use in ecclesiastical regulations.

The cultural settings of the biblical writings influenced not only statements about the natural world, but also social and religious statements. Although we might differentiate between religious statements and references to the natural world in the Bible, at the limit we find the partiality of even theological and ethical affirmations challenged by the fullness of the God of Jesus Christ and God's word disclosed through Scripture. At the same time, however, we recognize that it is through those culturally constrained affirmations that the fullness of the word is disclosed.

Those of us who want to allow that word to challenge us and to challenge every inadequate understanding of that word are put into the position of advocating biblical error in our struggle for truthfulness and dynamic biblical errantry. This is an actual reversal of our role that has taken place because the battleground was chosen by others. The statement of the thesis for discussion—either *error or the ancient dogma of inerrancy*—is chosen by those who advocate the older form of the dogma of inerrancy. The thesis for discussion in this chapter is *errantry or the ancient dogma of inerrancy*. Can a contemporary modern view of biblical inerrancy be formulated, a view that honors the authority and ever-contemporary relevance of Scripture?

Translation of the Doctrine of Inerrancy

How can we take the abstract and deductive statement on inerrancy that we have inherited from the ancient and medieval church (a doctrine that was satisfying in an earlier day) and transform it into a concrete and inductive doctrine that is consistent with our experience with the biblical text (and is satisfying today)?

We must begin with the understanding that any doctrine (whether the doctrine of inerrancy or any other doctrine) is always stated within a certain framework of thought. Paul's insight that "we have this treasure in clay jars" (2 Cor 4:7a) may be applied to the question of the relationship of the divine to the human in our understanding of the Bible. (Paul, of course is speaking of the weakness of the human body.) The reason for the treasure being in clay jars is "so that it may be made clear that this extraordinary power belongs to God and does not come from us" (2 Cor 4:7b). The ancient church began not "from below" in its understanding of the Bible. It did not look to the individual authors and historical contexts as a touchstone for meaning and truth of the Bible. The church began "from above." This practice cohered with the philosophical and theological system of thought that saw the visible world of phenomena as an exteriorization, an imperfect imitation of the intelligible world. This Neoplatonic worldview caused Augustine in his treatise on biblical interpretation (titled *On Christian Doctrine*) to declare that the properly prepared student who is spiritual and free will look beyond the sensible phenomena to the realities they express. Interpretation of the Bible was to issue in theological and ethical doctrine.

The ecclesial system of Augustine did not ignore the historical aspects of the Scriptures emphasized by later historical criticism. It relativized them or accommodated them to a different value or significance than did historical criticism. The massaging of biblical data and doctrine previously mentioned can be observed in Augustine. Augustine accommodated embarrassing historical reports in various ways depending upon the nature of the historical events. Apparently wicked actions of holy men and even of God could be rationalized by explaining the acts in light of circumstances prevailing in an earlier epoch. Polygamy, for example, was necessary in an earlier period to assure numerous offspring. A man's relationship with several wives was rationalized. A woman's relationship with several husbands could not be rationalized, however, because the woman would not become more fruitful as a result. "In regard to matters of this sort," Augustine declared, "whatever the holy men of those times did without lust, Scripture passes over without blame, although they did things which could not be done at the present time, except through lust." Actions or sayings that could not be so rationalized, that must be considered wicked under any circumstances, are to be seen as "wholly figurative, and the hidden kernel of meaning they contain is to be picked out as food for the nourishment of charity."[2] The allegorical method was the way of picking out the food to nourish charity.

Is a doctrine of inerrancy possible apart from the ancient Neoplatonic worldview and without the allegorical method? The world introduced with the Enlightenment was one that left Neoplatonism and allegory behind. The tools for research and the results of research had to accord with the new world. What was present but inert in the Ancient and Medieval Church—awareness of historically constrained authors and meanings of biblical writings and the historical nature of the events narrated—became the active theme in the historical-critical method.

History had to be given new weight. Biblical passages were given their full historical weight and not simply explicated as exteriorizations of the intelligible world, as
phenomena that could be unrelated to historical context as interpreted through
allegory.

The church *was* able to maintain a view of the authority of the Bible in light of
post-Enlightenment perspectives and approaches. In an early period of emphasis
upon "progressive revelation" and in a more recent period of emphasis upon the
action of God in history, the religious or theological message for the present day
was perceived in terms of development and progress. By the close of the nineteenth
century, biblical study was accommodated to historical study through the idea that
God revealed truth as humans were able to understand it. As Alan Richardson
observed:

> The conceptualization of "progressive revelation" enabled the enlightened and sen-
> sitive modern conscience to understand why it was necessary that the Bible should
> record the partial gropings and even the positive misconceptions of earlier ages;
> the Bible is the record of the religious education of the human race. . . . Every par-
> tial insight of Israel's long religious development was gathered, when at last men
> were prepared and able to receive it, into the final revelation of his truth which
> God gave to the world in Jesus Christ.[3]

This method of correlation was fully in accord with the spirit of the age, the
spirit of optimism and belief in the capacity of humans to realize their splendid
potentiality in the future. "Progressive revelation" as the key to understanding the
Bible was just as natural as belief in progress was the key to understanding history
and society. The historical method used in the framework of progressive revelation
accomplished for the nineteenth and twentieth centuries what the allegorical
method accomplished for the Ancient and Medieval Church: the reconciliation of
scriptural teaching with changing views of the universe and the rationalization of
ethical injunctions and practices that could no longer commend themselves to the
enlightened conscience.[4]

The challenge remains today to distinguish between the historical, sociological,
psychological, and scientific accuracy or inerrancy of individual biblical authors
and biblical books as historical products and the inerrancy or infallibility of the
authoritative religious message of the Bible as a canon of Scripture. The understanding that particular statements of the Bible make sense within the framework
of the Bible as a canon of Scripture remains important. Attention to contemporary
views of language and reading may help us in our quest. How do writings convey
meaning? How do readers make sense of writings? Words make sense as they join

together to form sentences, paragraphs, and larger literary units. A reader makes sense of the literary work by discovering some topic or theme that allows the words and sentences to fit together and form meaning. Words do not convey their meanings in isolation, but as readers see their relationships with larger linguistic units. This hermeneutical circle is helpful in understanding the relationship of the parts of the Bible to the Bible as a whole and (when all of the parts and factors are weighed) in explicating a contemporary view of inerrancy as well as errantry.

The whole Bible comprehends and supports the individual parts of the Bible. The individual sentences or even books do not stand by themselves. The inerrancy of the Bible has to do with the sentences, paragraphs, books, testaments, and layers of meaning piled upon one another in the development of the Bible. If we recognize that the meaning of a particular statement cannot be established apart from the whole system of reference within which it stands, and if we see the ultimate reference of the Bible as divine revelation utilizing but transcending culturally constrained references, then we can speak of a particular statement as being inerrant. It is only in this sense that we can conceive of the individual statements as being inerrant. When we take a word, a sentence, or a book out of context of the totality of Scripture and isolate it in itself (or place it in some other context such as history or philosophy or psychology), we cannot speak of the inerrancy of that word or sentence or book. A biblical text may not reflect what is now known historically or what is considered to be correct in terms of modern science, sociology, or psychology and yet still convey an authoritative word of God concerning our relationship with God and with people. In 1922, A. T. Robertson, the great Baptist New Testament scholar, attempted to direct attention of his readers from debates about historical and scientific facticity in an article on "The Bible as Authority" that appeared in the *Homiletic Review.*

> The essential problem about the Bible is not whether this detail of history has been established by research or whether this allusion in popular language to matter in nature is in harmony with modern scientific theory, which is constantly shifting its form of expression. That is quite beside the problem of the Bible. The authority relates to God's revelation of himself [*sic*] to men and to man's relation to God.[5]

The fact that biblical writers and biblical books reflect their culture and circumstances of origin is related to a dynamic errantry. To appreciate this we must give attention to the earlier discussion of the *way* words mean. The whole system of the Bible within which any word, sentence, or book stands has to do with what is being said by the words themselves. What is being said, however, does not make sense apart from what is *meant* by what is being said, meaning in the mind of the author but also meanings unconscious to the author and those implicit in the actual statements of the author. It includes meaning for today's readers, meaning for readers who actualize the biblical text in encounter with Christ in the life of the Body of Christ. Since the total system of reference of the Bible includes the reader who must actualize the biblical text, we may ask what meanings are allowed by a text for a reader or a generation of readers. With such a view, we are back to the Bible as a knight-errant, moving from generation to generation, bringing meaning for the readers and not simply antiquated original verbal and historical meaning. Original verbal and historical meaning is there, but not as a museum piece preserved and immutable.

Formulation of a Modern Doctrine of Inerrancy (and Errantry)

The doctrine of inerrancy requires a doctrine of errantry—a movement beyond the narrow historical circumstances of utterance. The concept of errantry embraces fully human writers—not semi-divine shades—and writings that are intelligible in particular historical contexts; it also embraces light and truth intelligible in the particular historical situations of our day. How is this wedding of inerrancy and errantry possible?

Another way of asking the question is to ask what John Robinson could have meant when he said that God has more light and truth yet to shine forth out of his word. I suspect we have believed that idea to mean gaining more and more information out of the Bible—just like getting more and more meat out of a hickory nut. Further information would result from more effective means of getting the meat out of the shell. The older dogmatic approach, for example, was incapable of getting all of the richness of the text, but the historical approach could obtain that richness.

It seems to me that a satisfying way of seeing what is implied in Robinson's statement is to see the Bible not as teaching a truth to which we get closer and closer as we develop better and better methods. Light and truth did shine forth for the ancients as well as for those in the new world of the Enlightenment. The light and truth of the Bible that shines forth for us is the light and truth made possible in our day in our particular situation. The Bible is seen, then, not as a finished and static collection of facts to be analyzed by increasingly sophisticated methods, but as a potentiality of meaning that is actualized by succeeding generations in light of their needs and by means of approaches supplied and authenticated by their worldviews.

We can see this errantry in the developing traditions of the Old and New Testaments. Seen from the perspective of a truth behind the text, or within the shell of the text, the progressive rewriting of the tradition risks the falsification of the truth or meaning. Biblical writers, however, were more interested in the relevance of the tradition for them and their generation. Is that not why Matthew and Luke rewrote Mark? I would argue that in our day we can continue the process that was begun in the Bible itself and has continued in the history of the reception of the Bible. Although approaches such as the dogmatic and the historical were productive in light of the worldviews that authenticated them, the errantry of the Bible today requires an additional move. A consideration of biblical texts from the perspective of literature will move us into a satisfying relationship with the Bible.

Contemporary readers of the Bible are discovering and creating relevant meanings through a literary or a literary-like reduction of the text paralleling earlier dogmatic and historical reductions. The literary reduction is accomplished against the horizon of earlier reductions and colored by those meanings; but by the nature of the literary reduction, something new becomes possible. I use the term "reduction" here not in a negative sense. In order to make sense of anything, we situate it, frame it, reduce it to "manageable" proportions. A literary or literary-like reduction, in fact (in contrast with other possibilities in our present context), allows errantry. Other approaches are governed by conventions that privilege truth as factual and that, therefore, are not able to embrace the principle of polyvalence that allows errantry. Literature, however, is governed by the polyvalence convention. This difference in approach increases the possibilities for readers to assign meaningful and personally relevant structures to biblical texts. The dogmatic approach reduced the text to dogma; the historical approach reduced the text to history. Those reductions were liberating in earlier days; now they are not totally satisfying. Today's reduction in light of literature will allow expansion of the text beyond narrow and to some extent currently unsatisfying dogmatic and historical dimensions.

How is it possible to conceptualize as literature with contemporary functions those biblical texts that originally had specific historically constrained purposes? I have three suggestions that I will outline briefly.

First, a contemporary reader may begin the process of seeing biblical texts in the light of literature by observing that the biblical writings did not originally function as technical theologies or histories.[6] If theology and history are not the only forms or genres in which to situate biblical texts, what is another genre that is satisfying today?

The answer to that question is to observe that biblical texts share with literary texts a use of language beyond the conventions of natural language. Biblical texts were composed originally in the Hebrew, Aramaic, and Greek languages, but they are also composed in the secondary languages or codes of imaginative literature. Poetry is widely used; and the prose of the Bible is frequently found in stories whose functions go far beyond those of scientific history. It is because of this literary use of language that the biblical text (as the artistic text in general) is filled with meaning. If the Bible were simply one-dimensional scientific writing, it would not be so quickly capable of errantry. Stephen A. Geller points out that biblical writers such as the prophets use language in the same fashion as poets, "manipulating its potentialities, consciously or unconsciously, to produce structures rich in meaning and forceful in emotion." Geller rightly condemns limitation of the poetic work of the prophets to dogmatic purposes. "How can one excise potential meanings if they are legitimate in terms of language and Israel's known system of beliefs and traditions? To declare that a poem may not be studied as such violates the principles of science, literature and language."[7] Literary aspects of biblical writings need not be mere superficial, ignorable characteristics. The biblical writings are designed for readers who will become involved with the writings as they become involved with literature, who will find and create meanings that involve them, that match their needs and capacity at cognitive and noncognitive levels.

After recovering the insight that the biblical texts are not histories or theologies in a strict sense and that they share characteristics of literature, what is to be done? In a second move, contemporary readers may investigate what is involved in reading biblical texts as literature. The distinction made by Aristotle between literature and history may be a starting point:

> It is not the poet's business to relate actual events, but such things as might or could happen in accordance with probability or necessity. A poet differs from a historian, not because one writes verse and the other prose . . . , but because the historian relates what happened, the poet what might happen. That is why poetry is more akin to philosophy and is a better thing than history; poetry deals with general truths, history with specific events.[8]

Aristotle's distinctions between history and literature may be restated as a direction to the reader. To read a text as history is to read it as a specific event, as what happened to particular individuals in geographically and temporally limited contexts. To read a text as literature is to read it as a universal truth, a truth relevant to us in our universe. Even those biblical texts that relate historical events in the lives of Israel, Jesus, and the early church were not composed pure and simply as objective history.

Biblical critics are so accustomed to the historical reduction that a conscious volitional act may be necessary to change the focus. An illustration of how a work that was originally intended to be history has become literature may be helpful. This has happened with Gibbon's *Decline and Fall of the Roman Empire*. Northrop Frye describes what has happened:

> In the first place, Gibbon's work survives by its "style," which means that it insensibly moves over from the historical category into the poetic, and becomes a classic of English literature, or at any rate of English cultural history. In proportion as it does so, its material becomes universalized: it becomes an eloquent and witty meditation on human decline and fall, as exemplified by what happened in Caesarian Rome. The shift in attention is simultaneously from the particular to the universal and from what Gibbon says to his way of saying it. We read him for his "style" in the sense that the stylizing or conventionalizing aspect of his writing gradually becomes more important than the representational aspect.[9]

Frye is describing what has happened in the history of reception of Gibbon's work, of course. But what has happened in the course of history may also take place in the conscious choice of individual readers. That is, a reader may choose to place biblical writings in a literary frame, emphasizing the style and the universal signification. Take Paul's letter to the Galatians as an example. It is a letter, a work of rhetoric. When we begin to appreciate the language and its manipulation as a rhetorical piece, we move away from dogmatic and historical frames of reference—at least as immediate frames. But may we do more? Is Galatians to be read simply as a historical document addressed to the ancient Galatian churches dealing with their historically limited problem? (For a brief period—but only for a brief period—the text existed as such a document.) Is it to be read as addressed to the Christian community in general dealing with the problem of Jewish law and Christian faith? (The Christian community imperceptibly made some such change as it continued to read the letter.) Can we read Galatians as addressed to believers of all persuasions who must reconcile the old and the new, or to humankind in general who face the challenge and threat of freedom?

By this time, a third step is necessary: a more serious questioning of the theological appropriateness of the literary genre for biblical writings. Is it legitimate to consider the Bible—a collection of religious writings—as literature? The conventional views of the roles and functions of literature and Scripture make mediation of literary and religious functions problematic. James Kugel says that he has "shuddered to hear it said that Joseph is 'one of the most believable characters in Western literature'" (that is, to subject the biblical text to literary criteria). His objection is

that "one wants to say that Joseph is no character at all but someone far more intimately ours."[10]

Does viewing the Bible as literature necessarily ignore the religious nature of
biblical texts? Kugel declares:

> The fact is, at a certain point these tales and songs, prayers and chronicles, began
> to be stitched together, first figuratively and then literally; *biblia* became a singu-
> lar noun and, among Christians, came to include both Old and New. This act, or
> series of acts, changed not only the text but as well the rules of literary compe-
> tence. For now not only were prophetic oracles and divine legislation invested in
> holiness, but everything associated with them, sagas, court histories, genealogies,
> songs, proverbs—all now, through a doctrine of divine inspiration, were associated
> by common authorship: one Book, one Author, and a special set of rules for read-
> ing it in keeping with its unique provenance.[11]

The narrow dogmatic view of the role and function of Scripture does preclude
the full appreciation of the Bible as literature. As we have seen, however, the view
that the Bible is designed simply to supply theological and ethical dogma is a historically constrained view and is not the only way to see the function of biblical
literature even in the church. In fact, the literary view advocated here supports the
possibility of "the ongoing canonization of Scripture," which is called for by Kugel
himself. Contemporary literary theory does not preclude "contamination" of the
literary by the philosophical, theological, and religious.

Although the uniqueness of the Bible is stressed, Kugel suggests that today's literary criticism of the Bible

> can indeed delight us and illuminate the text in surprising ways. Moreover, in
> seeking to bring together the work of different disciplines and sensibilities, the
> philologist's and the literary critic's, the Ancient Near Eastern historian's and the
> moralist's, our own day's criticism may yet perform an act of synthesis comparable
> in a more profound way to rabbinic writings, an act of *reading* in the contempo-
> rary sense, one which will address the complexity of the Bible's present dilemma
> and so take on the true calling of midrash, viz., the ongoing canonization of
> Scripture.[12]

A reader-oriented view of the role and nature of biblical texts as literature and an
application of strategies made available by contemporary criticism may perform
precisely the synthesis that is required for such an ongoing canonization.

Conclusion

We have come full circle and now see the relationship of the errantry and inerrancy of the Bible. Today, the Bible speaks most clearly not simply as ancient dogma or as the history of a tiny segment of yet more ancient people, but in an authoritative and convincing way as we utilize contemporary and satisfying theories and strategies to allow God's new light and truth to break forth. Contemporary reading that gives attention to the imaginative, creative, and religious needs of actual readers allows readers to recapitulate and correlate approaches that have been meaningful in the life of the church. Credulous approaches that seek to be obedient to a divine Word are included, as are critical approaches that seek to engage our intellectual capacities. Such reading will not only listen to the demands of contemporary biblical criticism, it will also carry out the mandate John Robinson gave the Pilgrim fathers.

Notes

[1] Daniel Neal, *History of the Puritans,* pt. 2, ch. 2, quoted in Ernest A. Payne, *The Fellowship of Believers: Baptist Thought and Practice Yesterday and Today* (Carey Kingsgate Press, 1952), 74.

[2] Augustine, *On Christian Doctrine,* 3, xii, 18, 20.

[3] Alan Richardson, "The Rise of Modern Biblical Scholarship and Recent Discussion of the Authority of the Bible," in *The West from the Reformation to the Present,* vol. 3 of *The Cambridge History of the Bible,* ed. S. L. Greenslade (Cambridge: Cambridge University Press, 1963), 314.

[4] The approach of "biblical theology" in America in the mid-twentieth century may be viewed as parallel to the approach of "progressive revelation." In the case of biblical theology, however, the emphasis was not upon progressive revelation of truth consistent with human capacity to comprehend such truth because the liberal view of human capacity had altered; the emphasis was upon the action of God in history. Rudolf Bultmann's existential reading of the Bible was satisfying for some. The existential approach examined the biblical text in terms of human existence and as a call to give up all worldly security for a new life that is lived out of the transcendent. In its mythical form of discourse the Bible tells us that in our everyday decisions we lay hold on our authentic being or lose it.

[5] Robertson, "The Bible as Authority," *The Homiletic Review* 83 (February 1922): 102.

[6] When this fact became known and accepted in biblical scholarship, of course, the historical model and method of study was so dominant that the texts continued to be studied as history with the focus being changed from the history of the events depicted to the history of those forming and transmitting the tradition and writing it down in final form.

[7] Stephen A. Geller, "Were the Prophets Poets?" *Prooftexts: A Journal of Jewish Literary History* 3 (1983): 219-20.

[8] Aristotle, *Poetics,* ch. 9.

⁹ Northrop Frye, *The Great Code: The Bible and Literature* (San Diego, New York, and London: Harcourt Brace Jovanovich, 1982), 46-47.

¹⁰ James Kugel, "On the Bible and Literary Criticism," *Prooftexts: A Journal of Jewish Literary History* 1 (1981): 219.

¹¹ Ibid., 233.

¹² Ibid., 234.

Chapter 3

Geography of the Bible

God's revelation of God's self in Israel and in Jesus the Christ took place among a people who lived in particular places on the earth—Palestine and the Middle East. Since the Bible grows out of God's self-revelation among God's people, these places must be of concern to the reader. The geographical locations within which the people of the Bible lived affected their lives and history, and knowledge of this geography will aid in understanding the Holy Scriptures.

General Geographical Setting

The world of the Old Testament and much of the New Testament was a rectangular area about 500 miles from north to south and 1000 miles east to west. Of course, the entire area was not inhabited because the desert, mountains, and sea limited the areas of occupation. James H. Breasted used the term "fertile crescent" to describe the inhabited area from the Persian Gulf up through the Tigris-Euphrates Valley and down into Syria-Palestine. The area is crescent-shaped. But Egypt, "the gift of the Nile," is also a part of the biblical picture. Perhaps the best way to picture the entire inhabited area of the rectangular portion described above is as a figure "S." If a figure "S" were drawn in the rectangle, the bottom arm would represent Egypt, the middle bar the land of Palestine, and the upper arm the Tigris-Euphrates Valley.

Geography of Palestine

The country of Palestine is the most important area in the biblical record. Christians are frequently amazed that the land of Palestine is so small. Its length is described in the Bible as "from Dan to Beer-sheba" (1 Kgs 4:25), a distance of only about 150 miles. The distances from east to west are even smaller. From Accho, in the north, to the Sea of Galilee is only 28 miles; and from Gaza, in the south, to the Dead Sea is only 54 miles.

The area is small but amazingly varied. Mount Hermon, just north of Dan, is 9,000 feet above sea level; much of the Jordan Valley is below sea level. The surface of the Dead Sea is lower than any other part of the earth's surface.

Geographers point out that Palestine is divided into four major parts: the coastal plain, the hill country, the Jordan Valley, and the Transjordan area.

The coastal plain. The Mediterranean Sea borders Palestine on the west and creates a long coastal plain running the entire length of the country. This coastal area was not as important for the Israelites as might be supposed, because the coast was not marked by many inlets or bays that could provide good ports.

The Plain of Philistia to the south is well known to Bible readers for it was the area of the coast where the Philistines settled early in the twelfth century BC. They gave their name to this coastal area and eventually to the whole land. The name "Palestine" is derived from the name "Philistine."

The hill country. Inland from the coastal plain was a range of hill country forming the backbone of Palestine. The hill country is of primary interest to Bible readers for it forms the well-known areas of Galilee, Samaria, and Judah.

Galilee is significant for New Testament study since Jesus' home was there and his early ministry centered in that area. Part of upper Galilee reaches a height of 3,000 feet, but lower Galilee is not so high and enjoys a milder climate and very productive soil. In lower Galilee are located Nazareth and the towns around the Sea of Galilee. It is against the background of lower Galilee, with its fertile basins growing grain, olives, and grapes, that the early life of Jesus must be pictured.

The famous valley of Jezreel separated Galilee from Samaria. This valley was on the most important road from north to south; therefore, the armies of Egypt, Assyria, and Babylon crossed it. Many famous battles mentioned in the Old Testament were fought there, and the Armageddon of Revelation 16:16 is pictured in the valley of Jezreel. South of Jezreel was the central hill country of Samaria with its famous mountains, Mount Gerizim and Mount Ebal. These mountains were sacred to the Samaritans, who built their temple on Mount Gerizim. This temple and mountain were referred to by the Samaritan woman when she told Jesus, "Our ancestors worshiped on this mountain, but you say that the place where people must worship is Jerusalem" (John 4:20).

The hill country of Judah was south of Samaria and contained the city of Jerusalem, by far the strongest city of Judah and the most important city of Palestine. Judah was more isolated, and hence easier to defend, than most areas of Palestine. The steep ascent from the Jordan and the barrier of the Dead Sea coast on the east, the hills on the west, and the desert on the south provided definite borders. The border facing Samaria was less well defined, and movement took place from one area to another.

The Jordan Valley. Running almost parallel to the hills of Palestine lies the great valley that is part of a giant geological fault running from Syria down to the Red Sea. Three bodies of water were located in this valley and were connected by the Jordan River: the Huleh Basin in the north, the Sea of Galilee a little further south, and still further, the Dead Sea.

The Transjordan area. Immediately to the east of the Jordan there were inhabited lands. To the north was Bashan, composed of fertile, wide, open plains that grew wheat in abundance. To the south of this land was Gilead, much higher than Bashan. The economic dependence of the people there was primarily upon the forest. The balm of Gilead is known to most Bible readers (Jer 8:22; 46:11). Still further south were the lands of Ammon, Moab, and Edom.

Beyond these inhabited areas was the Arabian Desert with its dry sands and hot sun that made regular habitation impossible.

The New Testament World
The New Testament world extended toward the west instead of the east. In fact, it was the world of the Roman Empire with its great political, cultural, and commercial centers. The two important areas for New Testament study, in addition to Palestine, are Asia Minor and the Greek lands. Both of these areas are important, for Paul and other early Christians traveled and wrote letters to churches located in them.

Asia Minor. Asia Minor was the bridge connecting southwest Asia with southeast Europe. This bridge has mountain ranges along the northern and southern edges with an elevated plateau between. Toward the west the mountain ranges draw near to one another and slope gradually down to the coast, opening into plains and river valleys that contain the towns familiar to Bible students. During the New

Testament period the Romans ruled Asia Minor and divided it into the provinces often referred to in the book of Acts and the letters of Paul.

Asia was the name of the province on the western seaboard of Asia Minor where the mountains slope into plains and valleys. (Do not confuse this relatively small area with the continent of Asia.) This Roman province of Asia contained the cities of Troas, Ephesus, Colossae, and Miletus mentioned in Paul's letters and travels. It also contained the cities named in the early chapters of Revelation: Ephesus, Smyrna, Pergamum, Thyatira, Sardis, Philadelphia, and Laodicea.

Cilicia is well known because it was the province in which Tarsus, the birthplace of Paul, was located. Bithynia and Pontus formed one province, but each part retained a certain individuality as is indicated by the divided name. It was into this area, located in the north of Asia Minor, that Paul attempted to go when he was directed by the Spirit of Jesus to go to Troas and on to Macedonia.

Galatia was the large central province. This Roman province contained the towns of Iconium, Lystra, and Derbe in which Paul ministered on his first and second missionary journeys.

Cappadocia was the province in the mountainous area east of Galatia and north of Cilicia. No missionary activity is recorded in this area in the New Testament times.

Macedonia and Greece. Macedonia provided the major land route between Asia and the west, including Rome. It became important in the biblical story when Paul journeyed from Troas across the Aegean to Philippi on the second missionary journey.

Macedonia had provided the initial stage for the activities of Philip of Macedon and his son Alexander the Great who united the Greek lands and spread the Greek Empire as far as Egypt and Babylon. In 148 BC it became a Roman province, and Thessalonica, one of the first cities Paul visited in Macedonia, was named as the seat of administration. The road Paul traveled from Philippi to Thessalonica was known as the Egnatian Way and was constructed by the Romans soon after Macedonia became a province.

Greece is known in the New Testament as Achaia. For a time (AD 15–44) Achaia and Macedonia were united into one province by the Romans, but just before Paul's activities in the Greek lands, Achaia had become a separate province with the seat of administration at Corinth.

As readers survey the history of the biblical people in the following chapter, they will benefit by reviewing this geographical setting and by frequently consulting maps of the biblical period.

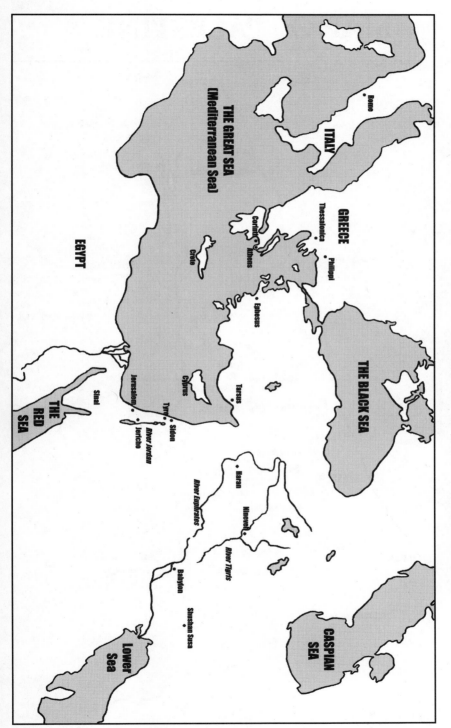

MAP OF THE BIBLICAL WORLD

MAP OF PALESTINE

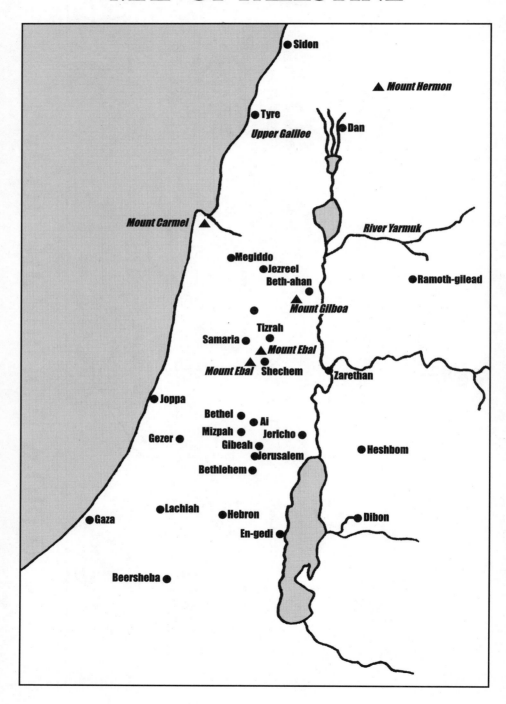

Chapter 4

History and the People of God

The 1963 edition of the *Baptist Faith and Message* confesses: "The Holy Bible was written by men divinely inspired and is the record of God's revelation of Himself to man." The affirmation that the Bible is a record of God's self-revelation was deleted in the 2000 edition because the committee on the *Baptist Faith and Message* felt that the Bible itself constitutes the revelation. History and historical reconstruction relativize the authority of the Bible as revelation. But the Bible as revelation presupposes and requires an understanding of God's self-revelation in human history. The 1963 edition of the *Baptist Faith and Message* is on target! Since the Bible contains a record about actual individuals in history who experienced and wrote of God's revelation of God's self, it is obvious that history is important. This chapter will present an overall survey of biblical history that will enable the reader to place the writings in their historical perspective. The chronological charts that follow provide detailed information to aid the careful student.

The Bible and History

The major events recorded in the Scriptures took place in a fairly limited section of the world over the course of about two thousand years. If the major developments over these years were considered as a giant play, the stage settings would be Palestine, the Nile Valley to the southwest, and the Tigris-Euphrates River Valley to the northeast. These locations were a center of civilization from the Stone Age to the Golden Age of Greece. Later, in the

New Testament period, the lands to the northwest of Palestine became a significant part of the stage.

When the biblical documents, beginning with the stories of the patriarchs in Genesis, are read against the background of early Middle East history (2000 BC), one major factor that influenced the entire history of Israel and the writings of both the Old Testament and the New Testament emerges. Palestine was a small country caught up in the procession of empires. Therefore, political independence was mainly a dream of the Israelites, and independence could be achieved only when there was a lull in the activities of the great states.

In addition to this general factor, applicable to nearly all of biblical literature, some of these books can be understood only with knowledge of the specific period of history that they reflect. Most of the books are better understood with some knowledge of their immediate historical background. The Bible gives only glimpses into the history of the Middle East. For comprehensive history, other sources must be sought. The materials uncovered by archaeologists in Egypt, Palestine, and the Tigris-Euphrates River Valley in the last century and a half are especially valuable. Some of these discoveries are discussed in the following chapter. Not until the twentieth century were materials uncovered and organized well enough for a real writing of the history of the Middle East.

History of Certain Nations

The Egyptians. These people of ancient civilization dominated the background first. The annual overflow of the Nile River created a great fertile area of land that made possible an early civilization in Egypt. About 3000 BC, one family in Egypt conquered all of the land and founded the First Dynasty.

While the patriarchs were wandering in the hill country of Canaan and the Negeb, the Egyptians were in control of Palestine and Syria. For a period (about 1720–1550 BC), foreign rulers seized control of Egypt and established a great empire that included Palestine and Syria; but about 1600 BC, these people were expelled from Egypt, and during the Late Bronze Age (1500–1200 BC), the native Egyptian kings sought to establish their authority over the northern area as far as the Euphrates River. It was in the last part of this period that the Israelites entered the promised land from Egypt.

When Egypt was in control of Canaan, a number of significant events occurred in the life of Israel that are recounted in the early Old Testament writings. The patriarchs lived a nomadic life in the hill country of Canaan for a time, but during a famine they moved into Egypt where they were welcomed and where they prospered. Later, the Egyptians enslaved them, probably by the new regime established after the expulsion of the foreign rulers. Under Moses' lead the children of Israel left Egypt, and under Joshua they entered into the promised land of Canaan. The early books of the Old Testament (Genesis, Exodus, Leviticus, Numbers, Deuteronomy, and Joshua) relate these events as refracted through faith and/or reflect the period during which they took place. (In using the chart, remember that not all the biblical books were written during the period that they reflect.)

Freedom from Egyptian control. During the beginning of the Iron Age (1200–1000 BC), the power of the pharaohs declined. Although Palestine remained nominally under the authority of Egypt, this authority was seldom recognized and enforced. For three centuries (1150–850 BC), Palestine was largely free from external control. This period saw the rise of the kingdoms of Edom, Moab, Ammon, Damascus, and the Philistine cities.

During this period of freedom from outside control Israel developed as a nation. As the Israelites settled in Canaan, they divided the land among the tribes and founded a religious confederacy. The new nation was subjected to invasions and border wars as well as occasional tribal strife within itself. This period of the judges is reflected in the books of Judges and Ruth.

In 1020 BC, the tribes were united into one kingdom with Saul as king. Under David and Solomon the kingdom prospered, but after Solomon's death, the empire divided into the kingdoms of Israel in the north and Judah in the south. The united kingdom and the divided kingdoms are dealt with in 1 & 2 Samuel, 1 & 2 Kings, and 1 & 2 Chronicles.

The Assyrians. The Assyrian Empire was the next to make itself known. Although Assyrian history began about 2000 BC with a governor residing in Ashur (from which the country receives its name), it was the Assyrian Empire of the ninth and eighth centuries that played an important part in Israel's history.

The Assyrian leader, Tiglath-pileser III (745–727 BC), led Assyria in conquest during the eighth century. He consolidated his borders to the east and north, then led his armies westward. His program was to divide the west into provinces, each with its own governor. He also instituted a policy of exchanging masses of the population of the conquered territory. This weakened nationalistic feelings and made the people feel less united. In 733–732 BC he conquered Philistia, took Galilee and Transjordan away from Israel, and destroyed Damascus. He left the greatly reduced Israel, as well as Judah, Ammon, Moab, and Edom, under their native rulers whom he required to pay tribute. It is evident from a survey of the Old Testament books that the Israelites were greatly influenced by the activities of Assyria in this period. For example, in 721 BC Sargon II (722–705 BC) destroyed Samaria for its rebellion.

In the next century, Assyria was desperately engaged in a struggle to hold its gains. Most of its energy was spent in defensive warfare against southern, northern, and eastern powers. The high point of the Assyrian Empire was drawing to a close, and Babylon, another world power, was about to exert itself.

The prophets Amos, Hosea, Micah, and Isaiah ministered during the Assyrian period of domination, and the books bearing their names must be studied against the background of this period. These prophets saw Assyrian power coming as punishment for the sins of God's people. Isaiah 10:5-6 is a vivid expression of this view:

> Ah, Assyria, the rod of my anger—
> the club in their hands is my fury!
> Against a godless nation I send him,
> and against the people of my wrath I command him,
> to take spoil and seize plunder,
> and to tread them down like the mire of the streets.

The Babylonians. Upon the death of the Assyrian leader Ashurbanipal in 626 BC, the Babylonians became the major power.

Babylonia received its name from Babylon, the major city of the empire, and like Egypt and Assyria it had a long history. The Babylonian Empire of this period is really Chaldean (controlled by nomads who had moved slowly into Babylonia and taken over the country), and it is frequently called NeoBabylonian to distinguish it from the earlier Babylonian Empire under Hammurabi. This new Babylonian Empire captured Ashur in 614 BC; then they attacked Nineveh, which fell in 612 BC. Ashur was the capital city earlier, but Nineveh had become the capital by this time. Nineveh was one of the oldest and greatest cities of Mesopotamia.

Palestine remained vassal territory during this period because there was no great leader to establish a coalition against the Babylonian king Nebuchadnezzar. Only Jehoiakim of Judah, with encouragement from Egypt, offered trouble. But as a result of this resistance, Judah was besieged and the young king Jehoiachin, son of Jehoiakim who died during the siege, was carried into captivity. A decade later Judah again rebelled, in spite of the strong protest of Jeremiah. At this time, 587 BC, the country was utterly devastated. Jerusalem with its temple was destroyed, and many people were deported to Babylon.

When Babylonia gained control of the empire of the Assyrians, the people of Judah were not unhappy. The core of the book of Nahum is a vivid poem extolling the destruction of Nineveh by Babylonia in 612 BC. "Nineveh is like a pool whose waters run away" (2:8), the writer declares.

> Celebrate your festivals, O Judah, fulfill your vows,
> for never again shall the wicked invade you;
> they are utterly cut off (1:15).

Jeremiah ministered before and just after the destruction of Jerusalem, and the book bearing his name must be read against that background. Several books reflect the destruction of Jerusalem in 587 BC and the exile after the destruction. Lamentations is a series of poems mourning the destruction of the city and the suffering of her people. It begins, "How lonely sits the city that once was full of people! How like a widow she has become, she that was great among the nations! She that was a princess among the provinces has become a vassal" (1:1).

The short book of Obadiah reflects the action of the Edomites at the destruction of Jerusalem by the Babylonians in 587 BC. The author says that the Edomites "should not have gloated over your brother on the day of his misfortune" (v. 12). But because Edom did, Obadiah declares that "shame shall cover you, and you shall be cut off forever" (v. 10).

The ministry of Ezekiel extended from before the exile to the middle of the exile in Babylon. The first twenty-four chapters are oracles of warning before the fall of Jerusalem. "For the land is full of bloody crimes; the city is full of violence. I will bring the worst of the nations to take possession of their houses. I will put an end to the arrogance of the strong, and their holy places shall be profaned" (7:23-24). But in the period of exile, Ezekiel declares that there is hope! "Thus says the Lord GOD: When I gather the house of Israel from the peoples among whom they are scattered, and manifest my holiness in them in the sight of the nations, then they shall settle on their own soil that I gave to my servant Jacob" (28:25).

The Persians. During the days of Babylonia's King Nebuchadnezzar, powerful empires existed to the east, north, and northwest of Babylonia. They needed only to be united to overthrow the Babylonians and establish a new empire. By 549 BC a Persian named Cyrus had united the people of his land, defeated one of the kings, and begun the Persian Empire. By 546 the capital of yet another state had fallen to Cyrus. Then Cyrus was ready to strike at Babylonia. In 539 he easily defeated the Chaldean army and entered into Babylon without opposition.

By 525 Egypt was added to the Persian Empire by Cyrus's son. Thus in the space of twenty-five years the whole civilized East as far as India was brought under Persian control.

The organization of the great empire was a colossal task brought to completion by Darius the Great (522–486 BC). He ruled Egypt and Babylonia directly and divided the rest of the empire into twenty provinces, each under a governor.

The Assyrian and Babylonian policy of deporting subject peoples was reversed by the Persians, and the exiled Jews benefited greatly from this policy. A large number of Jews returned to Palestine, built a new temple between 520 and 516 BC, and rebuilt the walls of Jerusalem under Nehemiah's leadership after 445 BC.

Chapters 40–66 of Isaiah reflect the period immediately before the fall of Babylon to Cyrus. The writer exults in anticipation of exiled Judah's return to Palestine.

Remember these things, O Jacob, and Israel, for you are my servant;
I formed you, you are my servant;
O Israel, you will not be forgotten by me.
I have swept away your transgressions like a cloud, and your sins like mist;
return to me, for I have redeemed you.
Sing, O heavens, for the LORD has done it;
shout, O depths of the earth;
break forth into singing, O mountains, O forest, and every tree in it!
For the LORD has redeemed Jacob, and will be glorified in Israel. (44:21-23)

The Babylonian Empire fell to the Persians under Cyrus in 539 BC. In 538, Cyrus gave an edict that permitted the Jews to return to their homes from bondage in Babylon. A number of Jews returned, and the books of Ezra and Nehemiah tell of their activities in rebuilding the temple and restoring their life in Judah.

The prophets Haggai, Zechariah, and Malachi were active in the period of restoration, and the books with their names must be studied against the background of this period of restoration.

The Greeks. In the fourth century BC, the center of political power moved westward, and Greece began to dominate the Mediterranean world. The competing city-states of Greece had recognized that Persia was a threat to them when Persia made several attempts to add them to the Persian Empire.

Alexander the Great carried on the war against Persia. This brilliant pupil of Aristotle the philosopher became a provincial governor at sixteen years of age, an able general at eighteen, and king at twenty. In 334 BC he crossed the Hellespont into Asia Minor and challenged Persia. Within a few years he mastered the Persian Empire, conquering Asia Minor, Syria, Palestine, Egypt, and moving on as far as India. He had planted Greek cities and Greek influence over this wide area.

At his death in Babylon, 323 BC, there was no logical successor to take over the empire. Therefore, Alexander's generals fought among themselves. Eventually one segment of the army, the Ptolemies, established itself in Egypt, and another segment, the Seleucids, established itself in Syria and the East. This was very important for Palestine during the "interbiblical period." For a time Palestine was under the control of the Egyptian segment of Alexander's successors. In 198 BC, however, Antiochus III, a Seleucid king, defeated the Egyptian forces and became master of Palestine.

The Greek empires influenced Palestine and the religion of the Israelites in many ways. The Hebrew Scriptures were translated into Greek for Greek-speaking Jews in Egypt and elsewhere. The Greeks usually allowed the Jews freedom in religious matters. A change came in this policy with Antiochus Epiphanes of the Seleucid Empire. His attempt to abolish the Jewish religion brought on the Maccabean revolt that won religious and political independence for the Jews for more than three quarters of a century.

The Romans. It is well known that the Roman Empire was dominant during the New Testament period. Pompey, the significant person insofar as Palestine was concerned, in 63 BC completed the work of taking over for Rome the eastern Mediterranean lands that included Palestine. The Roman power was then acknowledged by a series of provinces and client states that ringed the Mediterranean.

The empire itself is dated from the rise to power of Augustus in 27 BC. Before his death many provinces were added to the empire, and under succeeding emperors other areas were added. At its height, the empire included the whole Mediterranean world, from Britain south to Morocco, east to Arabia, north to Turkey and Rumania, and west along the Danube River to the Rhine. Although the empire did not reach its largest extent until AD 117 under the Emperor Trajan, the essential outlines of the empire were established by the beginnings of the Christian era.

By the time of Christ, the Romans had taken over Palestine, and each of the New Testament books must be viewed against the background of the Roman Empire. The power of the Roman Empire created a long period of peace in the large area of the world it controlled. But there was unrest also among some of the subjugated peoples. Both of these matters are important for an understanding of early Christianity and the New Testament writings.

The Gospels, of course, tell of the ministry of Jesus in Palestine, a land controlled by the Romans. Acts (a companion volume to the Gospel of Luke) carries the story of Christianity through the work of Paul within the Roman Empire and tells of his arrest and imprisonment in Rome.

Because of the relatively short period of time covered and the stable historical situation, most of the New Testament books reflect the same general historical background. However, some of the books, written toward the close of the New Testament period, reflect the Roman persecution of Christians. During his reign, Nero persecuted Christians, and the book of Hebrews may reflect this persecution or some other unknown to us. First Peter also was written to Christians undergoing persecution. Perhaps it was written from Rome after the outbreak of the Nero's persecution in AD 64. Revelation is a New Testament book reflecting a definite persecution. It is generally thought to have been written during the last of Domitian's reign as emperor from AD 81–96.

CHRONOLOGICAL CHART OF THE BIBLICAL PERIOD

I. THE PRE-PATRIARCHAL PERIOD

THE STONE AGE, beginning at least 100,000 years ago. Agriculture is in evidence in the Near East by the Middle Stone Age. Villages and pottery appear in the 6th–5th millennia.

THE COPPER AGE, 4th millennium. Writing developed in Babylonia by 3500 BC.

THE EARLY BRONZE AGE, 3rd millennium. The great states of Egypt and Mesopotamia emerge.

II. THE PERIOD OF EGYPTIAN DOMINANCE

General History	History of Israel	Biblical Books Reflecting Period
c. 3000 BC, Dynasty I begins in Egypt		Genesis
	2000–1700 BC, Wanderings of Patriarchs in Canaan	
1710–1570 BC, Hyksos domination of Egypt	1700–1300 BC, Sojourn in Egypt	
1570 BC, Egyptian resurgence		
	1280 BC, Exodus from Egypt	Exodus, Numbers, Deuteronomy
	1250–1200 BC, Conquest of Canaan	Joshua
c. 1190 BC, defeat of the Sea Peoples, settlement of Philistines on coast of Canaan	1200–1020 BC, Period of Judges	Judges, Ruth
1065 BC, end of Egyptian Empire		
		1 Samuel 1–8

III. PERIOD OF ISRAEL'S FREEDOM FROM OUTSIDE DOMINATION

General History	History of Israel		Biblical Books Reflecting Period
After breakup of empire, Egypt never regained her former dominance in Mediterranean world. Some forays made into Paletine and Syria and some intrigue against successive powers of Assyria, Babylonia, and Persia.	*1020–922 BC, United Monarchy*		
	Saul, 1020–1000		1 Samuel 9–31
	David, 1000–961		1 Samuel 16–31, 2 Samuel, 1 Kings 1–2, 1 Chronicles 10–29
	Solomon, 961–922		
	922–587 BC, Divided Monarchy		1 Kings 3–11, 2 Chronicles 1–92 Chronicles 10–36
	Kings of Judah	Kings of Israel	
	Rehoboam (922–915)	Jeroboam I (922–901)	
	Abijah (915–913)		1 Kings 12–22 deals with the Kings of the divided monarchy through Ahab of Israel and Jehoshaphat of Judah.
	Asa (913–873)	Nadab (901–900)	
		Baasha (900–877)	
	Jehoshaphat (873–849)	Elah (877–876)	
		Zimri (876)	
		Tibni (876–)	2 Kings 1–17 deals with the kings of the divided monarchy from Ahaziah of Israel and Jehoshaphat of Judah to the end of the Kingdom of Israel in 721 BC.
		Omri (876–869)	
		Ahab (869–850)	
	Jehoram or Joram (849–842)	Ahaziah (850–849)	
		Jehoram (849–842)	
	Ahaziah (842)		
	Athaliah (842–837)	Jehu (842–815)	Amos, Hosea, Micah, Isaiah 1–39
	Joash or Jehoash (837–800)		
	Amaziah (800–742)	Jehoahaz (815–801)	
	Uzziah (783–742)	Joash (801–786)	
	Jotham (750–735)	Jeroboam II (786–746)	
		Zechariah (746–745)	
		Shallum (745)	
		Menahem (745–736)	
		Pekahiah (736–735)	

IV. PERIOD OF ASSYRIAN DOMINANCE

General History	History of Israel		Biblical Books Reflecting Period
745 BC, Tiglath-pileser seized throne and ruled Assyria to 727 BC	Ahaz (735–715)	Pekah (735–732) Hoshea (732–722)	
724–722 BC, Siege of Samaria			
721 BC, Samaria falls to Assyrians	Hezekiah (715–687)		
701 BC, Siege of Jerusalem	Manasseh (687–642)		
	Amon (642–640)		
612 BC, Fall of Nineveh to Babylonia	Josiah (640–609)		Zephaniah, Nahum, Jeremiah

V. PERIOD OF BABYLONIAN DOMINANCE

General History	History of Israel	Biblical Books Reflecting Period
609 BC Battle of Megiddo	609 BC, Josiah killed at Meggido by Necho of Egypt	
605–562 BC, Nebuchadnezzar rules	Jehoahaz 609 Jehoiakim 609–598	
605 BC, Battle at Carachemish, defeat of Necho		
597 BC, First Deportation		
587 BC, Fall of Jerusalem		
	Jehoiachin 598–597 Zedekiah 597–587 587–538 BC, Judah in exile in Babylonia	Lamentations, Obadiah Ezekiel, Daniel, Isaiah 40–66

VI. PERIOD OF PERSIAN DOMINANCE

General History	History of Israel	Biblical Books Reflecting Period
539 BC, Fall of Babylonia to Persia with Cyrus as ruler		Ezra, Nehemiah, Esther
538 BC, Edict of Cyrus permitting Jews to return to Jerusalem		
	520–516 BC, Rebuilding of Temple	Haggai, Zechariah, Malachi
	458 BC, Mission of Ezra (some scholars date it in 428)	
	445 BC, Nehemiah becomes governor in Judea	

VII. PERIOD OF GREEK DOMINANCE

General History	History of Israel	Biblical Books Reflecting Period
333 BC, Battle of Issus, Persia falls to Greece		
331 BC, control of East by empire of Alexander begins	331 BC, Alexander at Gaugamela, beginning of Greek rule of Judea	
After Alexander were divisions, finally Ptolemies conrol Egypt and Seleucids control Syria	323–198 BC, Palestine under control of Ptolemies in Egypt	c. 250 BC, beginning of translation of Hebrew Old Testament into Greek
	198 BC, Battle of Panium, Seleucids gain control of Palestine	
	175 BC, Antiochus Epiphanes attempts to Hellenize Jews	
	167 BC, Maccabean Revolt	
	165 BC, religious freedom won by Jews, Temple Rededicated	
	142–63 BC, political independence of Jews	

VIII. PERIOD OF ROMAN DOMINANCE

General History	History of Israel	History of Christianity	Biblical Books Reflecting Period
63 BC, Pompey takes Jerusalem, Roman rule over Palestine begins	37 BC, Herod the Great becomes king of Judea		
31 BC, at battle of Actium Octavius (Augustus) defeats Antony and rules empire to AD 14	20–19 BC, Herod begins to rebuild temple in Jerusalem		
	4 BC, Herod's death, rule divided among three sons: Antipas (Galilee), Philip (Iturea), Archalaus (Judea)	5 BC, birth of Christ	Matthew 1-2 Luke 1-2
Roman Emperors after Augustus			
Tiberius, AD 14–37	Pontius Pilate procurator, AD 26-36	AD 26–28, preaching of John the Baptist	Matthew, Mark, Luke, John
		AD 27–30, ministry of Jesus	
		AD 30, crucifixion	
Caligula, AD 37–41		AD 35, conversion of Paul	Acts
Claudius, AD 41–54		AD 41–44, Peter imprisoned by Herod Agrippa	
		AD 44, execution of James, son of Zebedee	
		AD 47–48, Paul's first missionary journey	James
		AD 49–52, Paul's second missionary journey	1 Thessalonians 2 Thessalonians, Galatians
Nero, AD 54–68	Felix, procurator, AD 52-60	AD 53–58, Paul's third missionary journey	1 Corinthians 2 Corinthians, Romans
		AD 58, Paul arrested in Jerusalem	

General History	History of Israel	History of Christianity	Biblical Books Reflecting Period
		AD 61, Paul in Rome, later events unknown	Philippians, Philemon, Colossians, Ephesians
		AD 62, death of James, brother of Jesus	1 Timothy, Titus, 2 Timothy
Galba, AD 68	AD 66–73, war with Rome	AD 66–67, flight of Christians to Pella	1Peter, Jude, 2 Peter
Otho, AD 69			
Vitellius, AD 69			
Vespasian, AD 69–70	AD 70, Jerusalem and temple destroyed by Rome		Hebrews
Titus, AD 79–81			1 John, 2 John, 3 John
Domitian, AD 81–96	AD 90, Council of Jamnia		
Nerva, AD 96–98		AD 95, Domitian persecutes Christians	Revelation
Trajan, AD 98–117			
Hadrian, AD 117–135			

Chapter 5

Archaeology and the Bible

What Is Biblical Archaeology?

Sensational discoveries in Bible lands, such as the Dead Sea Scrolls in 1947, have helped popularize biblical archaeology. These discoveries and the interpretations of them have lead some people to think of biblical archaeology as something quite different from what it really is. The term "archaeology" comes from two Greek words (*archaios*, ancient, and *logos*, discourse) and designates the scientific study of the material remains of past life. The field for archaeology is the world. There are special branches for every region of the world—South America, North America, South Africa, England, Palestine—wherever humans have lived.

Biblical archaeology deals with the lands of the Bible and the material remains related to biblical peoples and events. It is, perhaps, the best-known branch of archaeology due to widespread interest in the Bible.[1] At the outset the purpose and limitations of archaeology related to the Bible need to be understood. Its purpose is not to prove or disprove the Bible. Research has often confirmed specific facts in the Bible record, but archaeologists do not begin with the objective of proving any particular point. Biblical archaeology provides a greater understanding of the times, events, and people recorded in the Bible. It unveils the past and relates it to the biblical narrative. In the process, it emphasizes the historical nature of Jewish and Christian faith. In the 1960s, after a period of intense interest and activity in biblical archaeology, a representative of the field said,

No one can understand the Bible without a knowledge of biblical history and culture, and no one can claim a knowledge of biblical history and culture without an understanding of the contributions of archaeology. Biblical events have been illustrated, obscure words defined, ideas explained, and chronology refined, by archaeological finds. To say that our knowledge of the Bible has been revolutionized by these discoveries is almost to understate the facts.[2]

Historical Sketch of Biblical Archaeology

The Bible lands constitute more than the country of Palestine. Egypt, Assyria, Asia Minor, Macedonia, Greece, and even Rome are related to the biblical narrative and constitute a valid interest for biblical archaeology. Palestine is of central interest in the biblical story because it was the land to which the people of Israel came from bondage in Egypt; it was the land of David and Solomon; it was the land of Jesus.

Scientific study of the material remains in the Middle East is not old. Before World War I, limited work was done in a very elementary way. But after World War I, the British, with a mandate over Palestine, established a department of antiquities. Excavation that had ceased with the war was quickly resumed. Developments greatly increased knowledge of the biblical world, which in turn enlarged our understanding of the Bible. By comparing the results of work in various areas of the biblical world, a clearer picture of Palestine and the ancient Middle East could be formed. W. F. Albright, an outstanding American archaeologist, felt that 1939 was a significant year for biblical archaeology: "The time had come to begin the preparation of real syntheses of ancient Near-Eastern history and civilization."[3] He declared that because knowledge of archaeological chronology had increased so rapidly during the previous decades, events and cultural activities in different lands could at that time be correctly dated and related to one another.

During and following World War II, archaeological activity continued and increased. Arab-Israeli hostilities stopped excavation in Palestine for a period, but with the ending of hostilities and the partitioning of Palestine, work resumed in Israel and Jordan. Today American archaeologists are busy in Israel, Jordan, and Cyprus. There is little or no American work in other areas of the Middle East although national schools of archaeology do exist—as they do in Israel, Jordan, and Cyprus.

Biblical Archaeology Discoveries: Written Documents

Archaeologists have uncovered a multitude of material objects in biblical lands, and scholars have worked diligently using them to illuminate the Bible and biblical history. This section will deal with important written documents that help illuminate the Bible.

Perhaps the most important contributions to our understanding of the Bible have been made through the discovery of certain written documents. Not all of them were brought to light by archaeological excavation; many were discovered by chance. But scholars have cooperated in studying all the documents and applying their knowledge to biblical study.

Babylonian Chronicle. The Assyrian and Babylonian kings maintained written records of their activities. Since they had important contacts with Israel and Judah during the Old Testament period, these countries are mentioned in the records kept by the kings. For the neo-Babylonian period an "unusually objective and reliable source"[4] is provided by the "Babylonian Chronicle."

The texts (on clay tablets) were found along with other historical records in the excavated cities of ancient Mesopotamia. The Babylonian Chronicle is important for its contemporary account of activities from about the time of Ashurbanipal's death to the fall of Babylon to Cyrus in 539 BC.

The Black Obelisk. What is claimed to be "the most important single monument for illustrating the Bible"[5] as well as the only existing portrait of a king of Israel was discovered in December of 1846 at Nimrud, a mound in ancient Assyria. This monument is the Black Obelisk and contains the annals of Shalmaneser III, a great Assyrian king. Of particular interest is a series of three panels showing Shalmaneser III receiving tribute from the Israelite king Jehu, son of Omri.

Moabite Stone. In 1868 a European missionary traveling east of the Dead Sea viewed a slab of black basalt. It was discovered to contain an important inscription telling of the wars and constructions of Mesha, king of Moab, in the ninth century BC. Although the stone was later broken up, a squeeze (a copy made by placing soggy paper on the inscription, which when dry retains an impression of the writing) was made before the destruction. The text tells of relations between Mesha and King Omri of Israel.

Siloam Inscription. On a hot June day in 1880, a young boy, playing in Jerusalem, waded in a pool of water south of the Old City. He was actually wading in a tunnel long known to archaeologists. Forty-two years earlier, Edward Robinson had found that the tunnel was the conduit for water from a spring to the north, and he believed that the tunnel ended in the Pool of Siloam mentioned in the Bible.

The young, native boy slipped into the waters of the stream, and when he came to the surface he noticed letters cut into the tunnel wall. News of the inscription spread. When scholars translated the writing, the inscription was discovered to be an ancient "plaque" describing the very work mentioned in the Bible (2 Kgs 20:20; 2 Chr 32:30).

Amarna Tablets. In the fall of 1887, a group of more than 300 clay tablets was found by an Egyptian woman who lived near Tell el Amarna (about two hundred miles south of Cairo). The tablets were sold to a neighbor who in turn disposed of them for a profit. Eighty-two of the tablets were purchased by the British Museum, but the remainder quickly spread throughout the world. This discovery, with the later discoveries of archaeologists, provided approximately 307 tablets containing Babylonian cuneiform. Cuneiform scholars quickly saw that the tablets constituted a file of the Egyptian foreign office during the reigns of two Egyptian rulers. These letters are a major source of knowledge concerning the history of Palestine and Syria during the early fourteenth century, for many of the letters are from rulers in important towns in Palestine and Syria.

Code of Hammurabi. In the last part of 1901 and the first of 1902, three large pieces of stone were discovered at Susa (one-time capital of Elam). When put together, these pieces formed a monument over seven feet high that was covered with columns of cuneiform writings and a scene of a king before the sun-god Shamash. This turned out to be a law code of Hammurabi containing about 250 laws and dating back to about 1792–1750 BC. Apparently, it had been carried away from Babylon to Susa after the time of Hammurabi.

This code is important as a source for knowledge of Babylonian daily life during the time of the Hebrew patriarchs. James B. Pritchard declares that it "has thrown more light on life in ancient Babylonia than any other single monument."[6]

Execration Texts. In 1926 a volume was published containing texts from broken pieces of pottery bowls that had been purchased at Thebes in Egypt by the Berlin Museum. The writings on the pottery were "execration texts," curses that apparently were to become effective when the pottery was smashed. On these bowls, and on fragments of clay figurines found later in Egypt, names of rulers, tribes, and cities are mentioned. Some towns mentioned in the Bible are also mentioned in these texts. Perhaps this practice is related to a practice recorded in Jeremiah 19:11-12.

Ras Shamra discoveries. In 1928 a Syrian plowman accidentally ran his plow into a large stone and discovered that it belonged to a tomb. This accident led to the discovery of a cemetery and a lost ancient city that was the most important Canaanite site archaeologists had found to that point. In May of 1929 a library of the ancient city was discovered. A few days later a number of inscribed tablets were uncovered. They were in an unknown cuneiform script—later deciphered and called Ugarit, after the ancient name of the town where the texts were found.

Ugarit has supplied invaluable materials for an understanding of the religious situation in Canaan before the Israelites came. The documents not only contain religious texts but also letters, commercial texts, schoolwork, and legal writings.

Lachish Letters. The Lachish letters, dating from the time of Jeremiah and addressed to a military officer (probably the commander of Lachish, a town in southern Palestine), were from a subordinate in charge of a northern outpost. The writing was on pottery and in the Hebrew language. The letters indicate the form that Hebrew correspondence took, show how ancient Hebrew characters were formed, and provide insight into the history of the crises years of the 580s BC.

The letters were found in debris from ancient Lachish. The first one was recognized on January 29, 1935, by some writing on a piece of broken pottery that was in material from a Persian roadway through a gate to Lachish. By the time all the letters had been discovered (much of the correspondence was never recovered, of course) about a hundred lines of Hebrew writing from the time of Jeremiah had been recovered.

Gnostic Writings. The Secret Sayings of Jesus is a book that promises something special for the followers of Christ.[7] It is an introduction, translation, and commentary on one of a collection of "Gnostic" writings accidentally discovered in 1945 or 1946 about 32 miles north of Luxor on the Nile River.

The 13 codices had been well preserved in jars (perhaps one very large jar), and nearly 80 of the 100 pages of manuscript were intact. The writing is Coptic (apparently a translation from Greek originals) and the materials date to the third or fourth centuries AD. Twelve of the volumes became the property of the Coptic Museum. The Jung Institute in Zurich, Switzerland, acquired one volume. This has become known as the Jung Codex and contains "The Gospel of Truth" that was translated in 1956. Later in 1956 the director of the Coptic Museum at Cairo made another volume public. Among other writings, this volume contains "The Gospel of Thomas," which was translated into English in 1958.

These writings show how one early group of Christians understood and reinterpreted Christ. The writings are not on a par with the New Testament writings.

They are later reflections on the meaning of Jesus and his message from the point of view of "Gnostics," a religious movement of the second century and later, which emphasized "knowledge (*gnosis*)" as a means of redemption.

Dead Sea Scrolls. The Dead Sea Scrolls were discovered in 1947 when an Arab shepherd accidentally found several manuscripts in a cave on the west shore of the Dead Sea. They eventually became the possession of the State of Israel, but war between the Arabs and the Israelis delayed a scientific investigation of the cave area. When an investigation was made early in 1949, several hundred fragments of biblical and nonbiblical writings were found.

Since then more scrolls and fragments have been found in the caves around the area, and nearby ruins that have been excavated show that the site was a large monastery that served as a center for a Jewish group living in the area.

Scholarly discussions have taken place on such questions as the date of the scrolls and the identification of the group that used them. By various means scholars have ascertained that the group was doubtless a segment of the Essenes (one of the major Jewish groups of New Testament times, discussed by Philo, Josephus, and Pliny) and that the scrolls date to the first century AD and earlier.

The Dead Sea Scrolls are important for a number of reasons. The Old Testament manuscripts discovered among the scrolls are nearly a thousand years closer to the time when the original books were written than are previously known manuscripts. They assist Old Testament textual criticism, especially by confirming the care with which the Hebrew text was transmitted. The scrolls and other material remains provide knowledge of a Jewish sect that existed in the time of Jesus, John the Baptist, and the early church. The background of the New Testament, therefore, is illuminated by these discoveries. The exact relationship of the Christian community to the Dead Sea community is still being studied.

Biblical Archaeology Discoveries: Important Sites and Areas of Thought

In *The Millennium Guide for Pilgrims to the Holy Land,* James H. Charlesworth of Princeton Theological Seminary listed what he considers the most important sites and areas of thought that have helped us significantly to understand the Bible. In his "short list," he cites three cities, four artifacts that can presently be seen in the Israel Museum, remains in Jerusalem, and Peter's house in Capernaum. He does not include Sepphoris in his "short list," but he does discuss the significance of Sepphoris in the text.

Charlesworth cites three cities—Dan, Hazor, and Megiddo—and the most important discoveries at each of the three.

Dan. Dan is located in the northern part of Israel, at the foot of Mt. Hermon near one of the major sources of the Jordan River. The city was originally called Laish, but when the tribe of Dan conquered the city, the name was changed to Dan. Excavations began at Dan in 1966 and have continued almost uninterrupted since that time. The archaeological discoveries at Dan may be correlated with the biblical information about Dan. Judges 18 gives a detailed description of the conquest of Laish (Dan) by the tribe of Dan. Archaeology has not revealed the sort of destruction implied in the account in Judges, but the appearance of a stratum of occupation characterized by pits implies a change in the material culture of the population with the arrival of the new inhabitants. The Danites probably lived in tents and huts and stored their food in the stone-lined pits that were dug into the earlier levels of occupation. Charlesworth is most interested in the discovery in Dan of Jeroboam's golden-calf temple. Jeroboam I (978–907 BC) led a civil war after the death of Solomon and won control of the northern territory ("Israel"). To compensate for the loss of Jerusalem, Jeroboam built shrines at the northern and southern borders of his kingdom—one at Bethel and one at Dan. Archaeologists have uncovered evidence allowing them to reconstruct the sanctuary that Jeroboam built at Dan. Charlesworth declares, "Historians can now, for the first time in more than two millennia, more adequately re-create the life of those worshipping the golden calf during the time of Jeroboam I."[8]

Hazor. Hazor was an important town in northern Galilee. It was at the crossroads of trade routes from north to south and east to west. The city is prominent in the story of the settlement of the land. The northern campaign of Joshua was provoked by a coalition of northern cities under the leadership of the king of Hazor. The ruins of Hazor were first excavated in 1928 and then more thoroughly over the course of several sessions from 1955 to 1969. Charlesworth relates the results of excavation at Hazor with biblical history:

> Archaeologists digging at Hazor prove that someone burned the large city precisely at the time Joshua is said to have burned it. Furthermore, the archaeological evidence shows a discontinuity between those who lived there before and those who lived there after the destruction. The earlier ones were urban; those who conquered had been semi-nomads. Archaeologists working in the Israel Museum, the Albright Institute for Archaeological Research, the Hebrew University, and in major universities around the world are convinced Hazor reveals that Joshua and the Hebrews conquered it and burned it around 1250 BC. After this destruction, the lower city was abandoned. Thus we have found the history behind Joshua 11.[9]

Megiddo. Megiddo is a city in the valley of Jezreel. It is important because it guards the paths through which the east-west road passes as it moves from the coast to the Jezreel valley. The north-south road, leading from Hebron and Jerusalem to Tyre and Sidon, also passes through Megiddo. Megiddo is mentioned frequently in the Bible—beginning with the Israelites' entry into the land (Josh 12). Eventually the Israelites gained control of Megiddo and the city came under Solomon's administrative organization (1 Kgs 4:12). Solomon fortified Megiddo along with Jerusalem, Hazor, and Gezer. A major excavation project by German archaeologists took place between 1903 and 1905. In 1925 excavation was revived under direction of American archaeologists and continued to the outbreak of World War II. Additional work has been carried out beginning in 1960. The results of excavation at Megiddo can be correlated with the history of the Middle East. Twenty strata have been uncovered, with stratum twenty representing the beginning of settlement on bedrock and stratum one representing the last period of settlement, in the Babylonian and Persian periods. The abandonment of Megiddo is probably is to be associated with the conquest of Palestine by Alexander the Great in 322 BC.

Charlesworth is most interested in stables and numerous palaces uncovered at Megiddo. A large fortress palace was probably built under the orders of Solomon and he (or probably a later king) was responsible for the stables. Charlesworth asked his readers to use their imagination as they consider the stables and the water shaft and tunnel:

> The stables are impressive. The complex has stables for about 492 horses. The first constructions seem to date from the time of Solomon, but most were built during the time of Ahab (871–852). It is easy to imagine horses drinking water or eating feed from the rectangular depressions dug out of the rock installations. One can imagine servants getting the horses ready for riding or attaching them to chariots for battle, business, or even pleasure.
>
> The water shaft and tunnel . . . was built sometime before the Assyrian conquest of 732 BC. The shaft is 75 feet deep and the tunnel extends 210 feet to the water. On the one hand it is easy to stand and admire the astounding engineering abilities of the Israelites. On the other hand, it is easy to imagine women descending to the bottom to draw water from the well, and then ascending with these vessels full of life-giving nourishment.[10]

Charlesworth lists four artifacts that can and ought to be seen in the Israel museum: an iron pomegranate from Solomon's temple, two tiny silver scrolls containing the Prayer of Aaron in Numbers 6:24-26, an ossuary (a stone box for human bones) on the side of which are the words "Joseph Caiaphas," and a rectangular stone with the name Pontius Pilate.

Iron Pomegranate from Solomon's Temple. The Temple of Solomon was completely destroyed, but an iron pomegranate has been recovered. This tiny ivory pomegranate was attached to a wooden baton. It contains an inscription in Hebrew dated from the mid-eighth century BC, which translates, "a sacred donation for priests in the house of the Lord." Charlesworth says, "It was used in Solomon's Temple in some cultic way. Conceivably it was waved by a priest when fruits including pomegranates, were placed on an altar. Perhaps a Levite held the baton to lead a choir, when he directed their chanting on the steps of the Temple."[11]

Silver scrolls with Aaronic Prayer. In a collapsed tomb on the western shoulder of the Hinnom Valley, archaeologists found two tiny silver scrolls. They saw that the Hebrew word for "Lord" appeared three times and they questioned the nature of the inscription. "The answer was riveting," according to Charlesworth. "Each contained the earliest version of the Aaronic prayer that is said today by Jews and Christians . . . . The silver scrolls antedate the biblical texts found among the Dead Sea Scrolls by about five hundred years. They are thus the most ancient portion of the Bible."[12]

Caiaphas's Ossuary. In the construction of a road south of the old city of Jerusalem, workmen discovered an ancient tomb containing a stone box for human bones. The name "Joseph Caiaphas" was found on the side of the ossuary. Caiaphas is the name of the high priest who examined Jesus and the name on the ossuary may be that of this high priest. Charlesworth says:

> The probability that this "Joseph Caiaphas" is the Caiaphas who was the high priest when Jesus was arrested increases when one turns to Josephus' account. He provides the first name of this high priest. The emperor Tiberius sent Velerius Gratus to be prefect over Judah. This Gratus "gave the high priesthood to Simon, the son of Camithus; and when he had possessed that dignity no longer than a year, *Joseph Caiaphas* was made his successor" (*Antiquities* 18.34). Thus we learn from Josephus that the high priest was called "Joseph Caiaphas"—the same first and last name as on the ossuary.[13]

Pontius Pilate inscription. While working on the amphitheater in Caesarea, archaeologists turned over a stone that had been used as a step and found a Latin inscription with the name of Pontius Pilate and his title "Prefect." Pilate was the prefect who condemned Jesus to be crucified.

Charlesworth lists three sites in Jerusalem that help in interesting ways in understanding the biblical narrative. These are Ophel (the city in which David lived), the broad wall of Jerusalem (Hezekiah's wall), and the Essene Gate.

Ophel. In his *Millennium Guide,* Charlesworth advises his readers that they are able to see the remains of the city in which David lived. This is not in the present walled Old City. It is south of that city and may be approached by climbing the stairs to the right of the Gihon spring. Charlesworth says that after pilgrims climb the stairs, they come to an entrance.

> Proceed ahead, and you will see the remains of houses occupied by David's con-
> temporaries. These houses are constructed of piled fieldstone. If you look closely,
> you will see a toilet. Slaves would empty its reservoir just like maids did through-
> out the world only 100 years ago. Stop to see some of the exposed walls of David's
> City. They are made of fieldstones and not the massive ashlars still hidden beneath
> the earth of the southeastern promontory of Jerusalem.[14]

Hezekiah's Wall. The present-day walls of the Old City date from the sixteenth century AD, and debates have taken place over the exact location of walls from earlier periods. Within the Old City, archaeologists found remains of an earlier wall, a wall that probably dates from Hezekiah's time, from the eighth century BC. Charlesworth declares, "This wall helps us estimate the extent of the city, and proves that the Upper City was occupied before Hasmonean times."[15]

Essene Gate. Charlesworth lists Mt. Zion and the Essene Gate as sites enabling us better to understand the biblical narrative. Mt. Zion is the name given to the southwestern portion of the Old City and the area outside Zion Gate. When Josephus describes the western wall of Jerusalem in the time of Jesus, he speaks of it extending from the Hippicus Tower through a place called "Bethso" to the Gate of the Essenes. From there it moves southwest and then east where it finally joins the eastern cloister of the temple (*Wars* 5.144-45). A gate has been unearthed on the extreme southwestern hill—beneath two other gates. The lowest gate is from the Herodian period and would have been the gate known in Jesus' time. Charlesworth suggests that it was called the Essene Gate because it was the gate through which Essenes would travel from Jerusalem to Qumran. More importantly, it was the gate used by hundreds of men to go to relieve themselves after the Sabbath.

Charlesworth follows the suggestion of Y. Yadin in his reconstruction of the situation. The Essenes were so strict that according to Josephus they would not "go to stool" on the Sabbath. "Thus," says Charlesworth, "they would need to wait from about 3:30 on Friday afternoon until about 7:00 Saturday evening; that is because Shabbat begins at sundown on Friday and ends after sundown on Saturday. Then, the Essenes could rush out together to the latrine or Bethso (*beth-tsoa* means 'latrine'). This weekly phenomenon would have made an impression on those who lived in and near Jerusalem."[16]

Charlesworth cites other possibilities that allow pilgrims to relate the Mt. Zion area to the history of the Christian movement.

> Most likely, Jesus celebrated the Last Supper in the southwestern section of Jerusalem. Does that suggest some relation between Jesus and the Essenes? According to early Christian traditions, Jesus' family eventually moved to Jerusalem and lived in this section of Jerusalem. A large mikva [ritual bath] has been discovered east of the two smaller mikva'ot [ritual baths]. Obviously, many men could have entered this mikva and become ritually pure again. Some scholars imagine that it is here that the many priests who became followers of Jesus were baptized . . . . Could the priests mentioned by the author of Acts [Acts 6:7] have been Essenes?[17]

Peter's house. The Gospels tell us that Jesus grew up in Nazareth but that he moved his ministry to Capernaum—hailed in the Gospels as Jesus' "own city." Charlesworth thinks that a house located in Capernaum may be the house of Peter in which Jesus taught. He summarizes the evidence:

> A house has been located that may well be the house of Peter in which Jesus taught. It is beneath a fifth-century octagonal church and has plastered floors and walls that prove that by the second century, and perhaps earlier, followers of Jesus worshiped here and seem to have believed that this house once belonged to Peter. Plaster and the lack of living utensils indicate that beginning in the late first century AD this house was used as a "house church." From the third to the fifth centuries pilgrims inscribed graffiti in Aramaic, Syriac, Latin, and Greek. In them Jesus is hailed as "Lord," "Christ," and "God." The name "Peter" is also found. Much of the earliest level has disappeared, since the restorations in the fifth century partly demolished Peter's house and the "house church" that had held the earliest "Christians."[18]

Sepphoris. Sepphoris is not mentioned by Charlesworth in his "short list" of sites that have "helped us significantly to understand the biblical narrative." Perhaps this is because Sepphoris is not mentioned in the Bible. It is located on the Roman road that led from the Mediterranean to the Sea of Galilee and was being constructed as the capital of Galilee when Jesus was living in Nazareth.

Charlesworth treats the claim that Jesus, because he was a builder, may have helped construct Sepphoris. "That makes sense, since the word 'carpenter' in Greek (Mark 6:3) really denotes any type of building activity and since Sepphoris was being constructed as the capital of Galilee when Jesus was living in Nazareth and perhaps before he commenced his public ministry."[19] Charlesworth quotes the conclusion reached by Richard A. Batey with approval: "The realization that Jesus grew up in the shadow of Sepphoris, a burgeoning Roman capital city, casts new light on the man and his message—light that changes the perception of Jesus as a rustic from the remote hills of Galilee."[20]

Values of Biblical Archaeology

If the purpose of biblical archaeology is not to prove the Bible, how can it help biblical study? The literary and other materials that have been discovered assist the Bible student in understanding the literature and history of the Bible in many ways.

Meanings of Words. The documents discovered make the Bible more intelligible by providing the previously unknown meaning of many words and phrases. For example, in Hosea 3:2 a word is used that does not occur elsewhere in the Old Testament.[21] The word is *lethech,* and is used for a particular measure of barley. Since the word appeared nowhere else, Bible scholars felt that the text was in error and should be changed. In two texts from Ugarit, however, the word was used as it was in Hosea—to describe a unit of dry measure—although the size was not definitely stated.

A Hebrew word, *miqweh,* occurs in 1 Kings 10:28 in a description of Solomon's trading activity, but the meaning of the word has been unknown. The King James Version translates the word as "linen yarn": "And Solomon had horses brought out of Egypt, and linen yarn: the king's merchants received the linen yarn at a price." The American Standard Version has "droves": "And the horses which Solomon had were brought out of Egypt; and the king's merchants received them in droves, each drove at a price." Assyrian records indicate that the word must refer to a place, Kue, in Asia Minor. This, therefore, is the translation of the Revised Standard Version: "And Solomon's import of horses was from Egypt and Kue and the king's traders received them from Kue at a price."

A group of names appearing in 2 Kings 18:17, Jeremiah 39:13, and elsewhere was translated in the King James Version as personal names of individuals—Tartan, Rabshakeh, Rabsaris, and Rabmag. Assyrian inscriptions show that these words are actually titles of Assyrian officials. Tartan is the "commander-in-chief," Rabshakeh is probably the "field marshal," Rabsaris is perhaps the "chief eunuch," and Rabmag is apparently some other high official.

In Proverbs 26:23 two words are found that give some trouble, *kesef sigim*. The King James and the American Standard Versions translate this phrase as "silver dross." The King James Version says, "Burning lips and a wicked heart are like a potsherd covered with silver dross." The Ugaritic texts contain a word, *kesapsigim*, which means "like glaze." No doubt this is the word found in Proverbs. The Revised Standard Version translates the verse, "Like the glaze covering an earthen vessel are smooth lips with an evil heart."

Illustration of Practices. Another important value lies in the illustration of laws, customs, and religious practices mentioned in the Bible. Many of these practices have been obscure.

In Deuteronomy 14:21, this command is found: "You shall not boil a kid in its mother's milk." There is no apparent reason for this law, and students have sought a logical explanation for it. A poem in the Ras Shamra literature contains a reference to the cooking of a kid in milk, and it is practically certain that this was a Canaanite religious rite. The law in Deuteronomy is a forceful way of telling the Israelites not to practice pagan religious rites.

In Genesis 16, Sarah gives her servant Hagar to Abraham in order that she might bear him a son. Is this an isolated case, or is this a common practice? The Code of Hammurabi contains evidence that this was a common practice. The code provides that a handmaid who has been given by a wife to a husband and has borne him children may not be sold. She may be made a slave. One of the documents (a marriage contract) from Nuzi also says that if the wife is barren she must provide another woman for her husband. When a child arrives as a result of this union, however, the wife cannot drive out the child, as Sarah drove out Ishmael (Gen 21:10).

The tablets from Nuzi also shed light on the theft of the teraphim by Rachel when she and Leah fled with Jacob (Gen 31:19). The tablets afford evidence that there was a connection between the possession of the family gods and the right of inheritance. Rachel wanted to be certain to secure for her husband the right to inherit the property of Laban.

When Hezekiah was "sick unto death" with a boil, the prophet Isaiah directed that he have a cake or lump of figs placed on the boil (2 Kgs 20:7; Isa 38:21). The Ras Shamra tablets reveal the significance of this direction by a record that lumps of figs were used as poultices for horses. The medical use of figs was not an arbitrary act of the prophet; it was a practice long recognized in the area.

Contribution to History of Bible Lands. Another major contribution of archaeology—from the study of unwritten objects as well as written documents—is the knowledge of the history of Palestine and its surrounding areas. Although the purpose of the Bible is not to give a comprehensive history of Palestine and her neighbors, a knowledge of the history of the Middle East does aid in understanding the Bible.

W. F. Albright declared that "there are few fields where the progress of discovery makes constant revision of handbooks and other aids to study more necessary than in Biblical research."[22] He further stated that it has been in our generation "that the progress of research has made real synthesis possible."[23] In 1940, Albright published *From the Stone Age to Christianity.* Since then many books have been written utilizing recent archaeological discoveries in reconstructing the history of the Middle East. As the history presented by the Bible is compared with the history presented by archaeology, several conclusions are reached as to the reliability of the Bible:

• *General Confirmation.* Archaeology confirms that the past presented in the Bible is compatible with the actual past known from archaeology. If the biblical materials were mere fiction, this fact would be exposed by the world dug up by archaeologists. When one begins with the hypothesis that the biblical world is a mere fictional construct, one is amazed with the correlation of the biblical world and the world uncovered by archaeological research. In an early period of archaeological study the factual correlation of the biblical world to the world dug up by archaeology was emphasized. In *What Mean These Stones?* Millar Burrows discussed many ways in which archaeology gives general confirmation to the Bible. He pointed out that the social customs uncovered in archaeological sources fit biblical stories of the patriarchal period. The topography of the narrative fits the findings of archaeology. The names of characters in the Bible, the names of non-Israelite gods, the general cultural and religious background, all accord with the knowledge gained from archaeological documents.

The general New Testament picture is also confirmed by archaeology. The book of Acts, for example, purports to show the developments within the Christian community from the death of Christ to Paul's imprisonment in Rome. In the nineteenth century some scholars were attracted to the theory that Acts was really written much later than the first century with second-century ideas superimposed upon the narratives. Sir William Ramsay, however, demonstrated through his research in Asia Minor that the political, geographical, and historical atmosphere of Acts is that of the first century.

• *Specific Confirmation*. Although every detail of the biblical account has not been confirmed by archaeology and some details have actually been called into question, many specific historical details have been confirmed.

In the cuneiform sources and lists of conquered cities made by Egyptian and Assyrian rulers there occur names of cities and countries that also occur in the early portions of the Old Testament. Burrows says, "Shiloh has been shown by excavation to have been unoccupied during the Late Bronze Age, occupied in the Early Iron Age, and destroyed at about 1050 B.C., exactly as required by the narratives of the Old Testament."[24] He continues, "Gibeah was burned at about the time indicated by the account in Judges 20. Samaria was built at a time corresponding to the statement that Omri established it as the capital of the northern kingdom. The examples of such confirmation which might be given are almost innumerable."[25]

In a Babylonian record is an extraordinary confirmation of an account in 2 Kings. The statement in 2 Kings is that Jehoiachin was taken out of prison by Nebuchadnezzar's successor Evilmerodach, "and he did eat bread before him continually all the days of his life, and his allowance was a continual allowance given him of the king, a daily rate for every day, all the days of his life" (25:29-30, KJV). In Babylonian tablets containing the names of people who were given regular allowances of grain and oil at the court of Babylon is the name of "Yaukin king of the land of Yahud."[26]

The New Testament is confirmed in many details. The accuracy of Luke 3:1 had been called into question. It states that Lysanias was tetrarch of Abilene when the word of God came to John in the wilderness. Lysanias died in 34 BC, and scholars, therefore, concluded that Luke was wrong. An inscription, however, has been discovered which shows that there was another and later Lysanias of Abilene, although the exact dates of his reign are not known.

As indicated earlier, Ramsay concluded that the book of Acts was written in the first century because the general picture of that century recorded in Acts was confirmed by archaeology. In addition, there are specific items in Acts that are confirmed by archaeology. In Acts 18:12 Gallio is named as the proconsul of Achaia; an inscription not only confirms this fact but also gives the approximate date. Luke uses some special terms for Asian officials: "politarchs" at Thessalonica and "asiarcbs" at Ephesus. The use is correct.

Care must be used in the employment of archaeological data to confirm specific points in the Bible. As early as the 1940s Burrows stated that "there are statements and stories in the Bible which cannot be reconciled with the course of events disclosed by archaeological discoveries."[27] And in 1985, D. N. Freedman (a prominent disciple of W. F. Albright) declared that Albright's expectation of setting the Bible firmly on an archaeological foundation "seems to have foundered or at least floundered."[28] In particular, he admits that archaeology "has failed to prove the historicity of Biblical persons and events, especially in the early periods."[29]

The greatest contribution of archaeology, then, is not the confirmation or non-confirmation of specific points. Rather, archaeology uncovers the evidence that enables scholars to reconstruct the conditions under which people lived in biblical times and to understand better the biblical world and faith that comes to expression in the biblical texts. When one begins with the assumption that the world of the Bible is pure and simply the ancient world as uncovered by scientific research, that assumption is challenged. The world of the Bible is a world informed by religious conviction that cannot be confirmed or falsified by archaeological discoveries.

Conclusion. Charlesworth claims that archaeology is important for understanding the Bible as a historical and theological document.

Archaeology helps re-create the world and the culture in which the biblical events occurred. Since archaeology offers data that can be dated reliably, say—for example—to the tenth century BC or to other centuries, including the first century AD, then the time oriented episodes in the Bible can be reconstructed....The chronological network is crucial: that is, the biblical record and the narrative help date scriptural events, and stratification (the layers of debris in a site) as well as the dating of *realia* (such as pottery) provides dates for archaeologists. The chronology of the Bible and archaeology meet and in that intersection the ancient story may be re-created with sensitivity and informed imagination...The chronological link between archaeology and the Bible is vital for understanding sacred scripture. That is true because the biblical authors claim that *God has been revealed in historical events.* Thus, the Bible is like—but more than—one of Herodotus' history books, and like—but more than—one of Plato's dialogues. It is more than history because it contains theological claims that demand the response of the reader... It is more than philosophical or theological treatises because it describes theology in terrestrial and historical events.[30]

Notes

[1] The work of archaeology in the lands of the Bible, of course, may have a broader focus than the Bible, the focus of culture in general. Syro-Palestinian archaeology as such, then, is a multidisciplinary study of remains left by various subsystems of the culture of Syria, Palestine, and the Middle East in general so as to elucidate the total complex cultural process. This comprehensive and essentially secular archaeological enterprise had its origins in a biblical archaeology that was concerned with the Bible

and biblical history. "Biblical archaeology" as a part of the more comprehensive discipline of "Syro-Palestinian archaeology" is different from the early discipline of biblical archaeology. In the early period the goal of biblical archaeology was seen by some leading archaeologists as setting "the Bible firmly on the foundation of archaeology buttressed by verifiable data" (D. N. Freedman, "The Relationship of Archaeology to the Bible," *Biblical Archaeology Review* 11 [1985]: 6). In particular, there was a goal of providing historical validation for the patriarchal and conquest periods.

[2] G. W. Van Beek, "Archaeology," *The Interpreter's Dictionary of the Bible* (Nashville: Abingdon Press, 1962), 1, 203.

[3] William Foxwell Albright, "The Rediscovery of the Biblical World," *The Westminster Historical Atlas to the Bible*, ed. George Ernest Wright and Floyd Vivian Filson (Philadelphia: The Westminster Press, 1945), 9.

[4] D. J. Wiseman, "Historical Records of Assyria and Babylonia," *Documents from Old Testament Times*, ed. D. Winston Thomas (New York: Harper, 1961), 46.

[5] James B. Pritchard, *Archaeology and the Old Testament* (Princeton: Princeton University Press, 1958), 142.

[6] Ibid., 206.

[7] Robert M. Grant and David Noel Freedman, *The Secret Sayings of Jesus: According to the Gospel of Thomas* (London: Collins, 1960).

[8] James H. Charlesworth, *The Millennium Guide for Pilgrims to the Holy Land* (North Richland Hills TX: BIBAL Press, 2000), 82.

[9] Ibid., 95

[10] Ibid., 184.

[11] Ibid., 154.

[12] Ibid., 155.

[13] Ibid., 156. In October of 2002, the discovery of an ossuary of James, the brother of Jesus, was announced in a Washington press conference by Hershel Shanks, editor of *Biblical Archaeology Review*. The ossuary is similar to the ossuary of Caiaphas. The James ossuary contains the inscription in the Aramaic language "Yakov [James], son of Josef [Joseph], brother of Yeshua [Jesus]." The very next month, the ossuary was exhibited at the Royal Ontario Museum in Toronto, Canada, at the same time that the Society of Biblical Literature met in Toronto. A special session of the Society was devoted to scholarly discussion of the ossuary. The consensus of scholars is that the ossuary dates from the first century AD and that at least the portion of the inscription referring to James and Joseph is original. But other questions remain: the provenance of the ossuary, the genuineness of the portion of the inscription referring to Jesus, and (assuming the genuineness of the entire inscription) the degree of likelihood that the James mentioned is the brother of Jesus of Nazareth. These will undoubtedly remain questions of scholarly debate.

[14] Ibid., 134.

[15] Ibid., 145.

[16] Ibid., 149-50.

[17] Ibid., 150.

[18] Ibid., 71.

[19] Ibid., 208.

[20] Richard A. Batey, *Jesus and the Forgotten City: New Light on Sepphoris and the Urban World of Jesus* (Grand Rapids: Baker Book House, 1991), 209; cited in Charlesworth, *Millennium Guide,* 208.

[21] These examples and others can be found in J. Phillip Hyatt's "Archaeology and the Translation of the Old Testament," *An Introduction to the Revised Standard Version of the Old Testament* (New York: Thomas Nelson and Sons, 1952), 49-56, and Millar Burrows, *What Mean These Stones?* (New Haven: A. S. O. R., 1941).

[22] Albright, "The Rediscovery of the Biblical World," 9.

[23] Ibid.

[24] Burrows, *What Mean These Stones?*, 281.

[25] Ibid.

[26] Ibid., 282.

[27] Ibid., 278.

[28] Freedman, "The Relationship of Archaeology to the Bible," 6.

[29] Ibid.

[30] Charlesworth, *Millennium Guide,* 5. William G. Dever has suggested that an archaeology that has expanded beyond an early "biblical archaeology" provides a broader context and contributes in three different ways to the elucidation of the Bible. First, archaeology brings back to life the ancient Middle Eastern setting so as to give the Bible a credibility, a flesh and blood reality. Next, archaeology documents the environmental, cultural, technological, and socioeconomic conditions in Palestine associated with changes the Bible explains religiously. The emergence of Israel in Canaan, for example, is understood by the Bible as a miraculous gift of Yahweh (Jehovah, the Lord) through the leadership of Joshua. Archaeology complements this religious perspective by uncovering a history of the ascendancy of Israel as part of a complex process of socioeconomic change. Finally, archaeology allows a look at popular culture and folk religion, aspects of the life of Israel that are only hinted at in the biblical record. For example, the religion of Israel reflected in the Hebrew Bible was supposedly Yahwistic, with a major distinction between the religion of Israel and the Canaanite fertility religions. The folk religion uncovered by archaeology, however, was highly syncretistic. These popular cults of ancient Israel are visible here and there in the biblical record, but they are revealed clearly by the archaeological record. William G. Dever, "Syro-Palestinian and Biblical Archaeology," *The Anchor Bible Dictionary*, vol. 1 (New York: Doubleday, 1992), 354-66.

Chapter 6

The Major Theme of the Bible

The writers of the biblical books are obviously not primarily interested in giving an account of the major historical developments of the nations. The events are mentioned indirectly (often as if the readers knew the events) in connection with the developments in the life of God's people. The concern of the writers is God's activity among God's people.

The Central Message of the Bible

The central message of the Bible is God's revelation of God's self and God's will. This message is not difficult to discover because it emerges at numerous places in the Scriptures themselves. Throughout the history of God's people God is made known in God's redemptive activity. The center of the message of the Christian Bible is Jesus Christ and what God has done, is doing, and will do for humankind through Jesus Christ.

Paul's sermon in Acts 13:16-43 is a good summary of the basic message of the Bible. The major theme is the activity of God among God's people and in Jesus Christ. Some specific points are made in the sermon.

1. God chose the patriarchs.
2. God made the people of Israel great during their stay in Egypt and led them out of the bondage of Egypt.
3. God bore with them in the wilderness.
4. God gave the people the land of Canaan as their inheritance.
5. God raised up judges until Samuel the prophet.

6. God then gave them Saul and David as kings.
7. Through David's posterity God brought Israel a Savior, Jesus, as God had promised.

This view of God and God's saving activity was not new. Deuteronomy 26:5-11 contains an ancient confession of Israel's faith.

> . . . you shall make this response before the LORD your God, "A wandering Aramean was my ancestor; he went down into Egypt and lived there as an alien, few in number, and there he became a great nation, mighty and populous. When the Egyptians treated us harshly and afflicted us, by imposing hard labor upon us, we cried to the LORD, the God of our ancestors; the LORD heard our voice and saw our affliction, our toil, and our oppression. The LORD brought us out of Egypt with a mighty hand and an outstretched arm, with a terrifying display of power, and with signs and wonders; and he brought us into this place and gave us this land, a land flowing with milk and honey. So now I bring the first of the fruit of the ground that you, O LORD, have given me." You shall set it down before the LORD your God and bow down before the LORD your God. Then you, together with the Levites and the aliens who reside among you, shall celebrate with all the bounty that the LORD your God has given to you and to your house.

This confession emphasizes God's activity among God's people, the sojourn in Egypt, the deliverance from Egypt, and the gift of the land of Canaan. (See also Deut 6:20-25; Josh 24; and Ps 78.)

For the early Christians, the central activity of God was not the exodus. It was Jesus Christ. They underscored him in their preaching. Of course, there was variety in the statements concerning Christ in the sermons of the early Christians, but certain themes that occurred over and over again were obviously considered central. (See Acts 2:14-39; 3:13-26; 4:10-12; 5:12-32; 10:36-43; 13:17-41; 1 Cor 15:1-7; and Rom 1:1-4.)

First, the early preachers saw God's activities in Jesus Christ as related to God's activities among God's people from the beginning, and also as related to their sacred Scriptures, our Old Testament. "In this way God fulfilled what he had foretold through all the prophets" (Acts 3:18).

The sermons then emphasized that the New Age was brought in through Jesus of Nazareth, God's Anointed One (Anointed One = Messiah = Christ). "Therefore let the entire house of Israel know with certainty that God has made him both Lord and Messiah" (Acts 2:36).

Next, some summary of Jesus' life, ministry, death, resurrection, and exaltation was given. ". . . God anointed Jesus of Nazareth with the Holy Spirit and with power . . . he went about doing good and healing all who were oppressed by the devil" (Acts 10:38).

Finally, the hearers were called upon to respond to God's activities in Jesus Christ. "Repent, and be baptized every one of you in the name of Jesus Christ so that your sins may be forgiven; and you will receive the gift of the Holy Spirit" (Acts 2:38).

An Outline of the History of Redemption

Imagine the overall story of God's redemption in the form of an hourglass with movement from top to bottom. Thus seen, all of God's mighty acts of salvation focus on Jesus Christ. For the Christian, the central point of biblical history is Jesus Christ, but certain activities lead to and flow from God's redemption in Jesus Christ. These activities relate the church to Israel and indeed to all of God's creation.

God created the world and has certain purposes for it. Humankind is created in the image of God and commanded to "be fruitful and multiply, and fill the earth and subdue it; and have dominion over the fish of the sea and over the birds of the air and over every living thing that moves upon the earth" (Gen 1:28). However, Adam and Eve wanted to be "like God, knowing good and evil" (Gen 3:5). So when humankind rebelled in pride against God, the need for redemption became apparent.

The plan for salvation through a particular people began with Abraham. God chose Abraham and his descendants. God blessed them, and they were to be a blessing to the world: "I will make of you a great nation, and I will bless you, and make your name great, so that you will be a blessing. I will bless those who bless you, and the one who curses you I will curse; and in you all the families of the earth shall be blessed" (Gen 12:2-3).

Although God chose Israel as the instrument of God's saving purpose, not all Israel responded in obedience to God. Threats to the purposes of God were found not only in external forces but also within Israel itself. Nevertheless, a portion of this people, the remnant, carried on God's purpose. "On that day the remnant of Israel and the survivors of the house of Jacob will . . . lean upon the Lord . . . . A remnant will return, the remnant of Jacob, to the mighty God" (Isa 10:20-21; see also Ezra 9:8, 15; Isa 11:11, 16; 46:3; Jer 23:3; Ezek 11:13-20; Amos 3:12; 5:3; Mic 4:7; Zeph 2:3; Hag 1:12-14; Zech 8:6, 11-12.)

Later, for Christian believers the hourglass narrowed even further to include Jesus Christ. "But when the fullness of time had come, God sent forth his Son, born of a woman, born under the law, in order to redeem those who were under the law, so that we might receive adoption as children" (Gal 4:4-5).

The story of salvation broadened from Jesus to the remnant of apostles and other early disciples. Jesus chose the twelve, and at Pentecost the Holy Spirit came upon a larger group. Then came the broader Christian fellowship—the church of Jesus Christ. The church has a mission to the rest of humankind—paralleling Israel's mission to the world. The church is a new Israel.

The vision of the New Jerusalem in the book of Revelation brings the New Testament to a close, and it gives an appropriate conclusion to the activities symbolized in the hourglass figure.

> Then I saw a new heaven and a new earth; for the first heaven and the first earth had passed away, and the sea was no more. And I saw the holy city, the new Jerusalem, coming down out of heaven from God, prepared as a bride adorned for her husband. And I heard a loud voice from the throne saying, "See, the home of God is among mortals. He will dwell with them; they will be his peoples, and God himself will be with them; he will wipe every tear from their eyes. Death will be no more; mourning and crying and pain will be no more, for the first things have passed away." (21:1-4)

The historical context of the Christian story of salvation helps contemporary readers deal more faithfully with the question of the relationship between Christians and Jews than did earlier generations of Christians. One way of reading the story just sketched is to see the church as superseding Israel. A supersessionist Christianity has no place for a continuing covenant of God with Israel. A Christianity that sees Judaism as God's covenant people into which Christians enter through Jesus Christ and which continues to live and function alongside her sister (or mother) is a more helpful way of reading the Bible.

Chapter 7

Language of the Bible

Many English translations of the Bible are available today. It is important to remember, however, that the books of the Bible were written before the English language even existed.

Old Testament Hebrew

The language of the Old Testament is Hebrew. There are a few Aramaic passages, namely Daniel 2:4-7, 28; Ezra 4:8–6:18; 7:12-26; Jeremiah 10:11; and a few scattered Aramaic words. The Hebrew language is quite different from languages with which we are most acquainted, such as Greek, Latin, English, and German.

Characteristics of Hebrew include how the Hebrews formed their alphabet, how they put letters together to form words, and how they expressed action in their verbs.

External features. Some traits impress themselves upon an observer at the initial glance. Hebrew was written from right to left; it is still read this way today in printed form. Thus, the Hebrew Bible in book form begins at what we consider to be the back of the book.

The Hebrew alphabet of Old Testament times consisted of twenty-two consonants. The reader of the King James Version of the Old Testament will find the Hebrew alphabet in Psalm 119. This psalm is an elaborate acrostic composed of twenty-two sections with eight verses each. In Hebrew, each of the first eight verses begins with the first letter of the Hebrew alphabet, each of the second eight verses begins with the second letter, and so on to the last letter of the alphabet.

In the Sermon on the Mount (Matt 5:17-18), Jesus referred to the smallest letter in the Hebrew alphabet when he said, "Till heaven and earth pass, one jot or one tittle shall in no wise pass from the law, till all be fulfilled" (Matt 5:18, KJV). This is a reference to the Old Testament, and the "jot" represents the smallest consonant of the Hebrew alphabet. The "tittle" represents the horn-like marks that distinguish some of the Hebrew letters. In Hebrew these are called "crowns," "thorns," or "points." The statement of Jesus is a graphic way of pointing to the significance of the Law.

Although vowels were not written in early times, they were obviously used in pronouncing the Hebrew. After New Testament times, Jewish scholars devised a written form of vowels so that readers could understand the writing with ease and accuracy. Various stages in the representation of vowels can be traced, but the vowel sounds that were finally established as standard are those worked out by the Masoretes (Jewish scholars) in the seventh to ninth centuries AD.

Hebrew words. Most Hebrew words are formed from roots containing three consonants, although a few are from roots of two or four consonants. It has been computed that the Hebrew language combined the consonants in a variety of ways to form about 2,050 roots and about 5,000 words in all. However, only about 500 of these words were used frequently.

The words formed in this way are concrete and vivid because nearly all Hebrew words express a physical action or denote a natural object. For example, the words translated "sin" come from roots meaning "to miss the mark," "to be crooked," "to break bounds." To the Hebrew, the word "heart" rarely means the physical organ. This concrete word refers to a number of things, including the emotions (Prov 27:11), the intellect (16:9), or the will (Ezra 7:10). The word for compassion is literally "bowels" in Hebrew (Gen 43:30). It suggests an emotion deep within the person. To speak of a "patient" person, the Hebrew would say "long of breath" (Prov 15:18; 16:32). On the other hand, the "angry" person is short of breath (14:17), and the obstinate person would be described as "hard of neck" (Isa 48:4).

Some expressions sound strange in English: "holy of holies," "Song of Songs," "King of kings," "to generations and generations." These expressions illustrate the fact that the adjective in Hebrew has no comparative or superlative form. The "holy of holies" is the most holy place; the "King of kings" is the greatest king. In addition, the Hebrew language has few adjectives and therefore makes use of expressions that sound strange in regular English usage. In Psalm 12:2, for example, the expression "diverse weights" is denoted in Hebrew by a "stone and a stone."

In Exodus 23:1, a false report is expressed as a "report of falsehood." In Genesis 17:7, an everlasting covenant is "a covenant of eternity."

The Hebrew verb. In the English language, the verb indicates that an action is past, present, or future. On the other hand, the Hebrew verb indicates action simply as completed (perfect) or not yet completed (imperfect). Normally, the perfect expresses past time, but colorful exceptions to this rule are the perfect of certainty and the prophetic perfect. The perfect of certainty is used when the speaker is certain of the outcome or has fully determined to make certain actions occur. In Genesis 15:18, God declares that the descendants of Abraham will receive the land. The sentence may be translated, "To your descendants I will give this land." However, the perfect is used and it could be translated, "To your descendants I have given this land." The prophetic perfect vividly portrays the speaker's confidence in the certain fulfillment of the promise. In Isaiah 9:1 there is a discussion of what God will do for God's people. This verse may be translated, "The people who walked in darkness shall see a great light." Again, since the perfect is used, it may be also translated, "The people who walked in darkness have seen a great light."

Although the tense system may be considered defective, compared to English the verb is versatile as a means of showing action to be intensive, causative, reciprocal, active, passive, or reflexive. The same root can be used to indicate various kinds of action simply by the addition of different vowels, prefixes, and suffixes.

This brief description of the Hebrew language indicates how we should read the Old Testament—as symbolic literature of the senses and emotions, not simply as complex literature of sophisticated logic and thought. We must understand and apply this fact in our study of the Old Testament.

Hebrew poetry. An inspection of recent translations of the Old Testament reveals that much of it is actually poetry. In the New Revised Standard Version, 40 percent of the text is in poetic form. Many books are almost entirely poetry: the Psalms, Job, Proverbs, the Song of Songs, and Lamentations. Large sections of poetry are also found within other Old Testament books.

General knowledge of poetry helps us interpret the poetry of the Bible, but at least one aspect of Hebrew poetry must be explained, since it is not a characteristic of English poetry. A chief characteristic of all poetry is rhythm. A series of words or sounds is given, and the reader expects another series to follow that more or less corresponds to the original series. In classical and most popular poetry, the units are sounds. The poet considers the length of syllables, the stress upon them, and related matters. In older forms of poetry, however, the unit is not a sound but an idea. This is true in Accadian and Chinese poetry. It is also true of classical Hebrew poetry. In this form, the poet makes a statement that arouses an expectation. To meet the expectation, the poet goes back to the beginning and says the same thing or follows a line of thought parallel to the thought already presented. T. H. Robinson, in a study summarizing forty years' study of the poetry in the Old Testament, says that a fundamental principle of Hebrew verse form is that "every verse must consist of at least two 'members,' the second of which must, more or less completely, satisfy the expectation raised by the first."[1]

The opening words of Psalm 19 are a good illustration of parallelism:

> The heavens are telling the glory of God;
> and the firmament proclaims his handiwork.

Parallelism may actually take a number of forms. One obvious form is synonymous parallelism. This occurs when the theme is stated in the first member, then restated with variation in the second member. The second line is simply another way of saying the same thing as the first. For example:

> Happy are those
> who do not follow the advice of the wicked,
> or take the path that sinners tread,
> or sit in the seat of scoffers (Ps 1:1).

> The earth is the LORD's and all that is in it,
> the world and those who dwell in it (Ps 24: 1).

A second form is antithetic parallelism, in which the second member states the truth of the first in a negative form or offers a contrast.

> For the LORD watches over the way of the righteous,
> but the way of the wicked will perish (Ps 1:6).

A complementary parallel is formed when the thought of the first line is completed in the second line. Psalm 121:2 does this:

> My help comes from the LORD,
> who made heaven and earth.

In emblematic parallelism, the second member reproduces the thought of the first by means of a metaphor or a simile. An example of this is Psalm 1:4:

The wicked are not so,
but are like chaff that the wind drives away.

Stair-like parallelism may involve more than one line. It occurs when one member (or part of a member) in one line is repeated in the second, and made the starting point for a fresh step. An obvious example of this is found in Psalm 29:1-2:

Ascribe to the LORD, O heavenly beings,
ascribe to the LORD glory and strength.
Ascribe to the LORD the glory of his name;
worship the LORD in holy splendor.

Combinations and modifications of the forms mentioned are used throughout the poetry of the Old Testament.

The New Testament also contains parallelism. One interesting example is in the Lord's Prayer. The New Revised Standard Version places Matthew 6:10 in poetic form:

Your Kingdom come.
Your will be done,
on earth as it is in heaven.

Some scholars interpret the second line as repeating the idea contained in the first line; the coming of God's kingdom involves at least partly God's will being done on earth as it is in heaven.

F. F. Bruce declares that "much of the vivid, concrete, and forthright character of our English Old Testament is really a carrying over into English of something of the genius of the Hebrew tongue."[2] He points out that "biblical Hebrew does not deal with abstractions but with the facts of experience. It is the right sort of language for the record of the self-revelation of a God who does not make himself known by political propositions but by controlling and intervening in the course of human history."[3] God does impart to humankind a knowledge of God's self. God does so most effectively in terms of human life and human language. Therefore, we must understand that human life and that human language.

New Testament Greek

The New Testament, even documents written by Jewish Christians, was written in Greek. There is some evidence that portions of the New Testament originated in

Aramaic (a dialect closely related to Hebrew), but the documents of the New Testament are written in Greek and must be studied from the viewpoint of the Greek language.

Greek is a more familiar language than Hebrew because Greek and English are in the same language family. Many English words are directly or indirectly derived from Greek. The Greek alphabet was derived at a fairly early date from the Phoenicians. In the New Testament period, there were twenty-four letters in the alphabet. At least two of these letters are familiar by their use in the book of Revelation. "'I am the Alpha and the Omega,' says the Lord God, who is and who was and who is to come, the Almighty" (Rev 1:8). Alpha is the first letter in the Greek alphabet, and Omega is the last.

Koine Greek. The Greek of the New Testament is not the same as the Greek of Plato and Aristotle, who lived from three to four hundred years before Jesus was born. Less than a century ago, classical scholars had no distinct idea of the kind of Greek that appeared in the New Testament. The discovery of the place of the New Testament in the history of the Greek language is far more than just an interesting story. The results of the discovery play a large part in the interpretation of the New Testament.

Out of a renewed interest in Greek writings in the seventeenth century, the question of the purity of the Greek of the New Testament arose. Some scholars attempted to demonstrate that the Holy Spirit so inspired the New Testament writers that they wrote as pure a Greek as any classical author. Others thought that the Greek of the New Testament was a special Christian language inspired by the Holy Spirit. Some tried to show that the peculiarities of the New Testament Greek were due solely to the influence of the Hebrew idiom. One problem in determining the nature of New Testament Greek was the lack of other writings with which to compare the New Testament writings.

During the nineteenth century, papyri remains were discovered accidentally. Papyrus was a type of writing material used extensively in New Testament times, and these materials provided a clue to the solution of the problem of New Testament Greek. In the late nineteenth century, scientific excavations uncovered additional papyri remains written in the Greek language. Prior to this discovery, understanding of the Greek of the New Testament period was sought mainly from literary writings, as opposed to nonliterary, or vernacular, writings. A further problem existed because writings contemporary with the New Testament were colored by an artificial revival of the classical Attic dialect.

While reading some of the papyri edited by Bernard Grenfell and Arthur Hunt, Adolf Deissmann, a German pastor and scholar, saw that the Greek of the papyri was similar to the Greek of the New Testament. The more he studied, the more he saw the likeness, and he soon concluded that the Greek of the New Testament was basically the nonliterary or vernacular Greek, *koine* (or common) Greek.

It will be seen later that the Greek of the New Testament is a particular form of koine Greek, but Deissmann's discovery opened the door for grammatical study that continues in the present day. Deissmann's work provided evidence that the New Testament was written in a simple style that the ordinary reader could understood. The translator who presents the New Testament in a simple style, therefore, is being most faithful to the original writings. Minute differences that seemed more significant among the "literary" writers of an earlier period should not be belabored.

Influence of Semitic Language and Literature. Jesus and the earliest disciples spoke Aramaic. The Aramaic or Hebrew background of the primitive Christian movement influenced the sort of Greek used in the New Testament. In places, the Greek text itself is meaningless apart from an understanding of the Hebrew background. We are to understand the titles and names applied to Jesus from a Hebrew, not Greek, background. The Greek name for Jesus had the same meaning as the Hebrew word for Joshua—"savior." *Christ* is a Greek word meaning "anointed one," and it means the same as the Hebrew word translated "messiah."

Also, it is well known that Jesus designated Simon the apostle as "Peter," from a Greek word meaning "rock." However, the term "Cephas" is an Aramaic word meaning exactly the same thing as the Greek word "Peter."

The writers of the Gospels were aware that every reader might not understand their Hebrew or Aramaic words, so they frequently translated certain words: "'We have found the Messiah' (which is translated Anointed)" (John 1:41), and in the next verse, "'You are to be called Cephas' (which is translated Peter)."

Hebrew influence was further extended by the Greek translation of the Hebrew Old Testament. Through the conquests of Alexander the Great and those succeeding him, the Greek language and culture spread throughout the Middle East. As early as the middle of the third century BC, the Jews in Alexandria, Egypt, began a translation of the Hebrew Old Testament into Greek. The product of their work is called the Septuagint (from the word *septuaginta* meaning "seventy") because of the ancient tradition that seventy elders were responsible for translating the Torah into Greek.

Important concepts and words from this Greek translation of the Old Testament are used in the New Testament. Hence, some of the words in the Greek New Testament can be understood only from their Hebrew backgrounds. The process may seem complicated, but observe how it works. The English word "church" in the New Testament is derived from a Greek word, *ecclesia*. In the Septuagint the word *ecclesia* is used to translate a Hebrew word *qahal*. The basic meaning of *qahal* is "meeting" or "gathering." The term is used in Deuteronomy to describe the assembly that came before God on Horeb when God sealed a covenant with them—the people of God. This was the most significant use of the word *qahal* (*ecclesia*) in the Old Testament. The word defined the significance of the assemblage of Israel. The Jewish Christians, familiar with the Septuagint, could not fail to relate the *qahal* of God in the Old Testament and the *ecclesia* of God in the New Testament. The church is the people of the Lord.

The English word "Lord" in the New Testament translates the Greek word *kyrios*. In classical Greek the term *kyrios* means "lord," "master," "owner," "possessor." It was also used as a title of address, "sir." *Kyrios* is found throughout the Septuagint. It is used to translate the Hebrew word *Yahweh*, or "Jehovah," the name for God in the Old Testament. Therefore, when the early Christians referred to Jesus as "Lord," they frequently meant more than "sir" or even "master." They acknowledged that in Jesus Christ they had experienced the sacred.

The New Testament writers quoted from the Greek Old Testament as well as from the Hebrew Scriptures. In the New Revised Standard Version, Matthew 1:23 is translated, "Look, the virgin shall conceive and bear a son, and they shall name him Emmanuel." Matthew is quoting from Isaiah 7:14. In the New Revised Standard Version, Isaiah 7:14 is translated, "Look, the young woman is with child and shall bear a son, and shall name him Immanuel." This translation results from the fact that the Hebrew word in Isaiah 7:14 simply means "young woman." She may or may not be a virgin. In contrast, Matthew quoted from the Septuagint in which the Greek word used definitely means "virgin."

New Testament Greek as Greek. Although the Greek of the New Testament is not the same as the earlier classical Greek, an understanding of some aspects of the Greek language is helpful to a student of the New Testament.

It was noted that in Hebrew verbs there is no emphasis upon time, and action is treated as complete or incomplete. In Greek, time is involved in the tense, but tense refers primarily to kind of action rather than time of action. Action may be regarded as continuous. This kind of action is expressed by the imperfect tense, by most occurrences of the present tense, and by some uses of the future tense. Action may also be regarded as taking place at a point in time (punctiliar). Such action is regarded as a totality no matter how long the actual action may take. The aorist tense, many examples of the future tense, and a few uses of the present tense convey punctiliar action. In this matter, a little learning is a dangerous thing. Even a superficial knowledge of Greek tenses, though, will help readers use good biblical aids more intelligently.

First John 3:9 is one passage in which an understanding of Greek tenses is necessary to understand the message: "Those who have been born of God do not sin." In the first verse of the second chapter, the writer declares, "My little children, I am writing these things to you so that you may not sin. But if anyone does sin, we have an advocate with the Father, Jesus Christ the righteous." The tense of the verb "to sin" in 3:9 is the present, "be a sinner," not the aorist, "commit a sin." It refers to continuous action, not a specific act. Therefore, there is no contradiction. Charles B. Williams clarifies this passage: "No one who is born of God makes a practice of sinning."[4] He translates the first verse of chapter 2: "My dear children, I am writing you this so that you may not sin; yet if anyone ever sins, we have One who pleads our cause with the Father, Jesus Christ, One who is righteous."[5]

The Greek language has specific forms for conditional sentences. The forms used may indicate that the condition has been met, that it has not been met, or that it may be met. In Matthew 12:28, Jesus is quoted as saying to the Pharisees, "But if it is by the Spirit of God that I cast out demons, then the kingdom of God has come to you." The Greek form makes it obvious that the "if" clause is a fact and is better translated "Since it is by the Spirit of God." John 15:22 is translated "If I had not come and spoken to them, they would not have sin." The form of this sentence indicates that the condition is not true. Jesus had in fact come. They do have sin.

This chapter does not contain a comprehensive discussion of Hebrew and Greek grammar. It should, however, prepare readers to appreciate more fully the chapter on interpreting the Bible and assist readers to appreciate and understand more fully the English translations they use.

Notes

[1] Theodore H. Robinson, *The Poetry of the Old Testament* (London: Duckworth, 1947), 21.

[2] F. F. Bruce, *The Book and the Parchments* (London: Fleming H. Revell Company, 1953), 44.

[3] Ibid.

[4] Charles B. Williams, *The New Testament: A Translation in the Language of the People* (Chicago: Moody Press, 1950).

[5] Ibid.

Chapter 8

Literary Form in the Bible

Books are usually written by one author who uses a single form of writing, such as the novel, poetry, or drama. A reader unacquainted with the Bible might naturally assume that the same thing is true of the Bible, that one author who follows one form of writing is responsible for the entire Bible. Consider the plight of one who tries to read the poetry of the Psalms, the preaching of Isaiah, and the letters of Paul as the same type of literature.

The Bible, in fact, is a collection of books written over hundreds of years by a variety of writers using different forms of writing. The major forms used are historical narrative and other forms of narrative, prophecy, apocalyptic writing, wisdom literature, and letters.

Historical Books

Much of the Bible is in the form of historical narrative; it tells a story. In the books at the beginning of the Old Testament is a story of Abraham and his descendants from the early patriarchal period through the descent into Egypt, the exodus, the United Kingdom, the Divided Kingdom, the Babylonian exile, and the restoration.

The story in these books is limited to a particular group. The writers were not concerned primarily with the Egyptians, the Assyrians, Babylonians, or Persians. For example, Egyptian civilization was ancient by Abraham's time, but this civilization is not dealt with at length in the Bible. Extra-biblical sources must be consulted to reconstruct the history of Egypt. The biblical writers were concerned with Abraham and his descendants—the people of God. Additionally, the stories are not even comprehensive histories of God's people. For example, extra-biblical sources record events in the lives of the Israelites that are not included in the Scriptures. The religious history is of greatest significance!

The historical books of the Old Testament contain both event and interpretation. The writer of the book of Exodus is interested in more than the fact that a small group of Jewish slaves escaped from Pharaoh. The writer (and the religious community that kept the works and passed them on) was interested in these people because they descended from Abraham, with whom God made a covenant, and because God had led them from bondage to the promised land.

The first five books of the New Testament are also historical. Each of the four Gospels tells of Jesus Christ and covers the same basic period of time—the days of his earthly life. Acts, the second volume by Luke (the Gospel of Luke is the first), continues the story from the resurrection of Christ through the development of the Christian movement for the next three decades. Again, it is important to realize that the history in these books is a particular kind of history. It is not a treatment of all the events and peoples in the time of Christ. It is not even a complete and objective history of the man Jesus. The Gospel of John gives clear guidance for reading the Gospels: "Now Jesus did many other signs in the presence of the disciples, which are not written in this book. But these are written so that you may come to believe that Jesus is the Messiah, the Son of God, and that through believing you may have life in his name" (20:30-31).

We can consider the Gospels a record of events in the life of Jesus designed to give people knowledge of Christ as Savior and the desire to follow him as Lord. Acts shows how the gospel moved from the geographical context of Jerusalem and the religious context of Judaism to become what it was in reality—a universal gospel for all people.

Prophetic Books

A number of Old Testament books are called "prophetic" books because they contain writings reflecting the work of the prophets. Before we can understand this literature, we must understand the nature and work of the prophet. The classical period of Hebrew prophecy began in the middle of the eighth century BC with the appearance of Amos. Although there were earlier prophets such as Nathan, Elijah, and Micaiah, only the writings of the prophets beginning with Amos presently exist. These prophets were individuals who spoke the word of God. The Hebrew term translated "prophet" is *nabi*, and scholars generally agree that this Hebrew word is related to words meaning "to call" or "to announce." The prophet is one called by God and one who announces the purpose and activity of God.

The prophet has frequently been misunderstood in the belief that the prophet was simply a "fortune-teller" able to foretell the future. It is believed that the prophets looked into the future and predicted coming events according to God's timetable. Although some Old Testament prophets made predictions, their primary task was to speak to their contemporaries about the meaning of events in which they were involved. The major message of the prophets may be summarized in three points: Israel has forsaken God; the judgment of God upon Israel is inescapable; God's redemption, however, lies beyond the judgment.

Apocalyptic Literature

Two books in the Bible—Daniel and Revelation—and sections of several others— Ezekiel, Isaiah, and Joel—are related to the prophetic books, but they differ from prophecy. They are termed apocalyptic writings. The Greek word *apocalypsis* is a compound word meaning "an unveiling." The Greek title of the book of Revelation is "The Apocalypse."

A host of nonbiblical Jewish and Christian apocalypses provide the literary context for appreciating the canonical works. The canonical books follow the general pattern of the other apocalyptic writings, and some understanding of the noncanonical books helps us to understand the biblical writings.

Mitchell G. Reddish, in an interpretation of the book of Revelation, lists fourteen nonbiblical Jewish and twenty-three nonbiblical Christian apocalypses. He also discusses the characteristics of the literature. Reddish speaks of apocalyptic as "crisis literature." The writings were related to some critical historical situation, such as the persecution by the Syrian ruler Antiochus IV in the case of Daniel and by the Roman emperor in the case of Revelation. Reddish wrote, "The purpose of apocalypses was to give comfort and hope to people who were overwhelmed, confused, frightened, and beleaguered."[1]

Apocalyptic literature is generally of pseudonymous authorship. "In most apocalypses, the human recipient of the revelation is supposedly some important figure from the past. In actually, however, the author came later in history and wrote under an assumed name."[2] The book of Revelation does not make use of this convention.

The writers presented their messages as revelations of cosmic secrets to a human recipient. "These secrets usually involved information about otherworldly regions (heaven, hell, the places of the dead, the outer regions of the earth) and/or events of the final days (the destruction of the world, the Last Judgment, rewards for the righteous, and punishments for the wicked)." Dreams and visions are important elements of apocalypses. The otherworldly mediator "sometimes delivers the revelation orally, sometimes discloses it through dreams or visions, sometimes interprets the dreams or visions for the recipient, and sometimes serves as a guide to lead the recipient on a journey to otherworldly regions."[3]

The characteristic of apocalyptic literature that is most obvious is the predictive element. Apocalyptic writing pictured the present as a time of evil, turmoil, persecution, and upheaval. The future was predicted to be a glorious period of vindication, triumph, and freedom from all the handicaps that beset us here. The apocalyptic writers "refused to accept the present social and historical reality. The transcendent world that had been revealed to them presented clear evidence that in God's ultimate design, evil, pain, suffering, violence, and injustice do not belong. Through their visionary writings, the apocalyptic authors encouraged their readers to resist any worldview that was in conflict with God's ultimate goal for the world."[4]

Apocalyptic literature is filled with symbols. Reddish speaks of the book of Revelation: "Like no other work in the canon, the book of Revelation is filled with symbols and images that will titillate the imagination and cause the spirit to soar. It is a creative masterpiece that can invigorate, challenge, and inspire us. 'Blessed are those who hear and who keep what is written in it' (1:3)."[5]

In his delightful and instructive book, *Reading the Signs: A Sensible Approach to Revelation and Other Apocalyptic Writings*, T. C. Smith addresses the question of the relevance of apocalyptic literature today. He contrasts the relevance seen by those who are acquainted with Jewish and Christian apocalyptic literature and those who read only the books of Daniel and Revelation.

> For those who have studied Jewish and Christian apocalyptic literature and waded through its symbolism, there is nothing but praise and admiration for their attempts to cope with the problem of evil and the justice of God. For those who are acquainted only with Daniel and Revelation, these books become a draft for the predictions of the termination of the age. Little do they realize that these and other such works were written as tracts for the times. The writers did not have future generations in mind when they wrote. Their great concern was about persecution in their own day, and they looked forward to the time when God would break into human history and relieve them of oppression.[6]

Smith cautions against attempting to predict the consummation of history:

Those who get the apocalyptic fever and cannot endure the tension between the this-worldly and the otherworldly long for the consummation of history. The odds are perhaps a billion to one that they will die before this happens. Therefore, it is incumbent upon us to live the Christian life and leave the rest to God.[7]

Wisdom Literature

Three books in the Old Testament have been termed "Wisdom Literature" because they are the product of a distinct class, the wise men of Israel. These individuals were concerned mainly with the conservation and transmission of the community's accumulated wisdom. This was not the wisdom of formal religion; it was the wisdom that understood individual character and had insight into general human nature.

The book of Proverbs, the most obvious wisdom book in the Old Testament, is a collection of wise sayings designed to help the youth of its day achieve success and to avoid the snares and dangers inherent in living. Throughout the book a belief in rewards for personal merits and penalties for guilt is expressed.

Job, another wisdom book, challenges the theological presupposition that virtue is always rewarded in this life. Instead of being set forth as a series of wise sayings, the book is in the form of a drama in which Job and his three friends converse.

Ecclesiastes is a wisdom book in which the writer seeks to discover what is good for humans to do during the few days of their lives. Both humor and irony appear as the writer muses concerning folly and drink, commerce and arts, the nature of wisdom, the ways of human society, and other aspects of life.

Letters

The New Testament contains numerous writings in the form of first-century letters. Most of them are personal, written by Christian leaders such as Paul to specific Christian congregations and individuals. Paul sent the letter known as 1 Corinthians to the congregation at Corinth to answer a series of questions that had been asked of him and to solve certain problems that had arisen in the church. (See 1 Cor 1:11; 7:1; and 16:17.) He addresses such matters as factions in the church, church discipline, lawsuits in pagan courts, marriage, food dedicated to pagan gods, spiritual gifts, speaking in tongues, the nature of the resurrection, and contributions for the saints. It is obvious that Paul was writing a pastoral letter to a particular group with which he had had much contact.

Other letters of the New Testament were for more general reading. They are sometimes called "epistles." They dealt with more general truths and were addressed to Christians as a whole. The letter of James is such an epistle. It is addressed "to the twelve tribes in the Dispersion"—doubtless a way of saying "to all Christians who are living their lives in this world." There are no specific references that would be more pertinent to one congregation than to another.

Just as different standards for interpreting diverse forms of modem literature are used, so must various standards of interpretation appropriate to the different literary forms of the biblical writings be applied.

Figures of Speech

Understanding the thought of any ancient writer is challenging enough when translating ancient words into modem speech. The task is even more challenging when translating biblical writings, because the writers used words both in their ordinary sense and figuratively. In most cases, we can assume a writer intends the literal meaning of a word unless there is good evidence of an intention for figurative language. However, all possible resources must be consulted to uncover the truth.

Hebrew writers characteristically drew upon the experiences of their lives in Palestine as shepherds and farmers and used the language of everyday life to convey their greatest thoughts. For example, the Psalms abound with similes and metaphors.

The righteous who are "like trees planted by streams of water" (1:3) and the wicked "like chaff that the wind drives away" (v. 4) are etched in our memories because of the psalmist's use of figures of speech.

The condition of the individual in Psalm 22 is unmistakably clear: "But I am a worm, and not human; scorned by others, and despised by the people" (v. 6). The psalmist continues:

Many bulls encircle me,
strong bulls of Bashan surround me;
they open wide their mouths at me,
like a ravening and roaring lion. (vv. 12-13)

When the deliverance of God came to the writer of Psalm 18, he chose most appropriate words to describe God. He calls God a "rock," "fortress," "deliverer," "shield," "horn of my salvation," and "stronghold."

Who can forget the "shepherd" of Psalm 23? Even twenty-first-century readers who know nothing of the shepherd and his sheep are encouraged and made confident in God through the symbolic language of this psalm.

The prophets used picturesque language to proclaim their messages. The word picture painted by Amos of a frustrated Israel facing the judgment of God would be humorous had the truth not been so tragic:

> It is darkness, not light;
> as if someone fled from a lion,
> and was met by a bear;
> or went into the house and rested
> a hand against the wall,
> and was bitten by a snake. (5:18-19)

Certainly, we could not leave Amos without also listening to his message of consolation: "'I will plant them upon their land, and they shall never again be plucked up out of the land that I have given them, says the LORD your God" (9:15).

The vast majority of the figures of speech came from the daily experiences of the Hebrew people. This fact is a guide for understanding the writings. Read and reread the biblical writings until the regular background becomes a matter of general knowledge. A Bible dictionary will be helpful in understanding little-known terms.

Short figures. Short figures are encountered throughout the Bible. Often the meaning of the figure is evident, especially if the literal meaning of the word is known. The figurative meaning grows naturally out of the literal meaning. For example, the activities of a shepherd with his sheep make it natural for a sheep-raising people to call God shepherd.

The simile is a frequently used figure. One thing is described in terms of another with "as" or "like" added to give the idea of comparison. It is assumed that what follows the "as" or "like" is known to the reader and therefore will assist the reader in understanding the meaning. The description in Isaiah's vision vividly pictures the city of Jerusalem: "And daughter Zion is left like a booth in a vineyard, like a shelter in a cucumber field, like a besieged city" (Isa 1:8). It is obvious that neither Jerusalem nor the land of Israel is literally a booth or a shelter. In this case conjecture is unnecessary, for the writer expresses the truth literally when he says, "Your country lies desolate, your cities are burned with fire" (v. 7).

In Isaiah's description of the nations fighting against the people of God, the multitude of all the nations will be

Just as when a hungry person dreams of eating
and wakes up still hungry,

or a thirsty person dreams of eating
and wakes up faint, still thirsty. (29:8)

A stronger figure of speech is the metaphor. It is like the simile, but the "as" or
"like" is omitted. Jesus said, "I am the bread of life" (John 6:35), "I am the gate for
the sheep" (10:7), "I am the good shepherd" (v. 11). These are metaphors, more
powerful than similes would have been here: I am like the gate, I am like the good
shepherd.

Jeremiah describes the sins of the Israelites by use of metaphors:

Be appalled, O heavens, at this,
be shocked, be utterly desolate,
says the LORD,
for my people have committed two evils:
they have forsaken me,
the fountain of living water,
and dug out cisterns for themselves,
cracked cisterns,
that can hold no water. (2:12-13)

In reading biblical comparisons, keep in mind the actual subject of the comparison and the image by which it is communicated. The image should add to the
statement but should not be confused with the real subject. Usually, there is little
difficulty in discerning the truth in the comparison, especially if the context is kept
in mind.

In the Bible, writers commonly substituted for a particular word another term
closely associated with it, referring to something or someone by naming one of its
attributes. For instance, "By the sweat of your face you shall eat bread" (Gen 3:19).
The word "sweat" is used to represent hard labor. The phrase "law and prophets" is
frequently found in the New Testament. The Jewish people used this expression in
New Testament times to refer to Old Testament Scriptures. (This figure of speech
is called a metonymy.)

At times, a writer will refer to a whole by naming one of its parts. This makes
the statement more concrete and meaningful. Micah describes the glorious future
of God's people, ". . . they shall beat their swords into plowshares, and their spears

into pruning hooks" (4:3). The prophet is declaring that war will become peace. Swords and spears will be changed, but much more! (This is called a synecdoche.)

Another way of presenting an idea more concretely is to treat it as being human, having personality, intelligence, and emotion. Psalm 114 is an excellent example of personification. It declares that when Israel went forth from Egypt, "the sea looked and fled, Jordan turned back. The mountains skipped like rams, the hills like lambs" (vv. 3-4).

Some expressions in the Bible would tend to make us think that the speakers and writers were not telling the truth if the use of figures of speech was not familiar. The Gospel of John ends with the declaration that "there are also many other things that Jesus did; if every one of them were written down, I suppose that the world itself could not contain the books that would be written" (21:25). In Numbers 14:8, the writer declares that the land to which the Israelites were going was a "land that flows with milk and honey." Jesus said, "Again I tell you, it is easier for a camel to go through the eye of a needle than for someone who is rich to enter the kingdom of God" (Matt 19:24). All of these passages contain hyperbole. This figure of speech is a conscious exaggeration by the writer or speaker to gain effect.

Another figure of speech—almost the opposite of hyperbole—is understatement or negative statement. It is used to heighten the action described. Thus, Acts 1:5 says that the disciples were to be baptized with the Holy Spirit "not many days hence" (KJV). Here the author actually means a very short time. When Luke describes a debate between Paul and Barnabas and the Jerusalem Jews demanding circumcision as "no small dissension and debate" (Acts 15:2), he meant for readers to appreciate the intensity of the debate. The affair as recorded in Acts 15 was one of the most important matters discussed by the New Testament church!

Irony is a figure of speech that expresses an idea exactly opposite to that declared by the language. Jesus used irony with the Pharisees. He said that they are like their fathers who murdered the prophets, then built tombs and adorned monuments for them. "Fill up, then, the measure of your ancestors" (Matt 23:32). Paul used irony to great advantage in shaming his critics. "Already you have all you want! Already you have become rich! Quite apart from us you have become kings!" (1 Cor 4:8).

Many more illustrations exist. The Bible contains almost every possible figure of speech, and textbooks dealing with them frequently use biblical references as illustrations.

Extended figures. The Hebrew writers' practice of using comparisons to clothe their teachings did not stop with short similes and metaphors of one or two words.

The writers extended the symbolic language in parabolic sayings and longer narrative parables. Proverbs 6:6-8 contains a parabolic saying:

> Go to the ant, you lazybones;
> Consider its ways, and be wise.
> Without having any chief,
> or officer or ruler,
> it prepares its food in summer,
> and gathers its sustenance in harvest.

Immediately after this saying, the writer makes an application: "How long will you lie there, O lazybones? When will you rise from your sleep?" (v. 9).

Ecclesiastes 9:14-15 is an example of a longer parable:

> There was a little city with few people in it. A great king came against it and besieged it, building great siegeworks against it. Now there was found in it a poor wise man, and he by his wisdom delivered the city. Yet no one remembered that poor man.

The application is made: "So I said, wisdom is better than might; yet the poor man's wisdom is despised, and his words are not heeded" (v. 16). (Other parables in the Old Testament are 2 Sam 12:1-14; 14:1-11; 1 Kgs 20:35-40; Isa 5:1-7; Ezek 17:3-10; 19:2-9, 10-14; 21:1-5; and 24:3-5.)

Jesus used parables much more frequently than the Old Testament writers did. Scholars disagree as to exactly how many parables are contained in the Gospels. The question arises because of the difficulty in classifying the parables. Are compounded metaphors and extended metaphors to be considered parables? Matthew 23:24 and Luke 6:38 are examples. Are parabolic sayings such as Luke 4:23 and Matthew 5:3 to be considered parables?

More important than the question of whether a saying of Jesus is an extended metaphor or a parable is the matter of how to interpret the parables. Frequently, parables are interpreted allegorically. Augustine, following a traditional method of interpretation, explained the parable of the good Samaritan (Luke 10:30-35) this way:

> *A certain man went down from Jerusalem to Jericho*: Adam himself is meant; *Jerusalem* is the heavenly city of peace, from whose blessedness Adam fell; *Jericho* means the moon, and signifies our mortality, because it is born, waxes, wanes, and dies. *Thieves* are the devil and his angels. *Who stripped him*, namely, of his immortality; *and beat him*, by persuading him to sin.[8]

Before Augustine finished, he dealt with christology, the church, Paul, the resurrection, and other matters of equal importance. C. H. Dodd says that Augustine's interpretation of the parable of the good Samaritan continued to the time of Archbishop Trench, and this writer heard it in a chapel service during his high school days.

But *is* Augustine's interpretation what Jesus intended to convey by the parable? It was told in response to a question that a lawyer asked about eternal life. Jesus answered that he was to love God and to love his neighbor as himself. The lawyer, "wanting to justify himself, said to Jesus, 'And who is my neighbor?'"

Then Jesus told the story of the good Samaritan (a member of a group hated by the Jews) and asked the lawyer, "Which of these three, do you think, was a neighbor to the man who fell into the hands of the robbers?" When the lawyer replied that it was the "one who showed him mercy," Jesus declared, "Go and do likewise." What more graphic way could Jesus have chosen to speak this truth than by the example of a member of a despised group considered by Jews to be racially impure! This taught the lawyer that no human being was beyond the range of his love. The law of love is radical and limitless.

Parables are figures of speech drawn from natural or ordinary life that arouse the interest of the hearer and present a basic point of comparison. In interpreting the parables of Jesus, it is important to remember the environment of Jesus' ministry and that he used a particular literary form to convey a truth. In an allegory, on the other hand, there is a particular meaning in each event or detail. Ephesians 6:10-17 is an allegory describing God's armor and the Christian's warfare. The girdle is truth; the breastplate is righteousness; the shoes, peace; the shield, faith; the helmet, salvation; and the sword, the word of God.

Notes

[1] Mitchell G. Reddish, *Revelation*, Smyth & Helwys Bible Commentary Series (Macon GA: Smyth & Helwys Publishing, 2001), 4.

[2] Ibid.

[3] Ibid., 3-4.

[4] Ibid., 5.

[5] Ibid., 3.

[6] T. C. Smith, *Reading the Signs: A Sensible Approach to Revelation and other Apocalyptic Writings* (Macon GA: Smyth & Helwys Publishing, 1997), 126.

[7] Ibid., 127.

[8] Quoted in C. H. Dodd, *The Parables of the Kingdom* (London: Nisbet and Company, 1936), 11-12.

Chapter 9

Formation of the Canon

Christians have not always had the convenient collection of writings now known as the Bible. Abraham did not possess the Old Testament, much less the entire Bible, since the books were written after his day. Paul possessed writings of the Old Testament but had no New Testament. The collection of sacred writings into the canon (authoritative collection) is an interesting and instructive story.

Although some people may think it blasphemy to believe that God worked through individuals in history to give humankind the Bible, the fact is that the development of the Bible was a slow process involving many individuals and groups. This does not diminish the value of the Scriptures. Rather, knowing the facts can increase our understanding of the Bible in God's plan of the ages and help us use the Scriptures more effectively in making God's will and way known.

Significance of Writings to Early Readers

No one should think that the biblical writers were unaware of the truth and value of their message. Nor were the first readers ignorant of the authority of the writings. From a human standpoint, the very preservation of the writings is evidence that the first readers considered them valuable. Of course, the writings of the prophets were not always accepted immediately by the people. Like the prophets' sermons, their writings were treated at first with scorn and contempt. Not only was Jeremiah's preaching ignored and despised by the people and rulers, but his writings were cut to pieces and burned by King Jehoiachin.

Jeremiah 36:4 records that "Baruch wrote on a scroll at Jeremiah's dictation." Baruch read the words of Jeremiah to the people, and then the king himself sent for the scroll.

> Now the king was sitting in his winter apartment (it was the ninth month), and there was a fire burning in the brazier before him. As Jehudi read three or four columns, the king would cut them off with a penknife and throw them into the fire in the brazier, until the entire scroll was consumed in the fire that was in the brazier. (vv. 22-23)

Yet there were disciples of the prophets, such as Baruch, who valued and preserved the writings; and in the time of exile the people began to heed the message of the prophets.

Paul's letters are an example of how the New Testament writings were received by the first readers. Their preservation is evidence of their value to the recipients. Paul was their friend and leader. Furthermore, he was convinced that his message in Christ was authoritative. Although he sometimes says, "I say—I and not the Lord" (1 Cor 7:12), at other times he declares, "I give this command—not I but the Lord" (v. 10). The general tenor of Paul's letters indicates that he speaks with authority as an apostle of Jesus Christ.

Development of an Old Testament Canon

A difference exists between accepting writings as valuable and accepting them as an authoritative canon of the Scriptures. Complete information concerning the development of a canon with sixty-six books is not found in the Bible itself, but the Bible does reveal some of the important steps along the way.

Law. Although the writings in our present canon were circulated earlier, the first book officially canonized by the people of God was discovered in the temple of Solomon in the eighteenth year of the reign of King Josiah (621 BC). Second Kings 22–23 tells of the discovery. In the eighteenth year of King Josiah, while the Jerusalem temple was being repaired, a "book of the law" was found in a collection box or in some rubbish about to be removed from the temple. The king had the scroll read to him, and "when the king heard the words of the book of the law, he tore his clothes."

Then the king directed that all the elders of Judah and Jerusalem should be gathered to him. The king went up to the house of the LORD, and with him went all the people of Judah, all the inhabitants of Jerusalem, the priests, the prophets, and all the people, both small and great; he read in their hearing all the words of the book of the covenant that had been found in the house of the LORD. The king stood by the pillar and made a covenant before the LORD, to follow the LORD, keeping his commandments, his decrees, and his statutes, with all his heart and all his soul, to perform the words of this covenant that were written in this book. All the people joined in the covenant. (2 Kgs 23:1-3)

Overwhelming reasons exist for believing that the book mentioned in this passage is basically the book of Deuteronomy in our Old Testament.

After the return from Babylonian exile, the Israelites enlarged their canon. The book of Nehemiah provides evidence, recording an experience that took place after the return of God's people. They had gathered together in the square before the Water Gate in Jerusalem, and Ezra the scribe brought the book of the law and read it in the presence of the people. From the passage in Nehemiah 8:1 and other references, and from later uses of the term "law," the conclusion has been reached that the first five books of the Old Testament were accepted by the Jews as their canon of the Scriptures around 400 BC.

Prophets. Nothing is said about the prophetic writings in Nehemiah's account, but these writings existed at that time. There is no account of the canonization of the Prophets as vivid as that concerning the Law. However, evidence exists to establish the certainty that within two centuries of Ezra's reading of the Law, the Prophets were accepted as canonical. In the prologue to Ecclesiasticus, an apocryphal Old Testament book, reference is made to "the Law and the Prophets and the others that followed them." By the time that prologue was written in 132 BC, the Prophets had status comparable to that of the Law. By the New Testament period, the term "the Law and the Prophets" referred to the collection of the Scriptures considered canonical by the Jews.

The Writings and the close of the canon. There is yet a third division of the Old Testament, the Writings. The prologue to Ecclesiasticus refers to these writings when it mentions "the others that follow" the Law and Prophets, but it was not until after the time of Jesus that the Jews gave "official" status to the Writings. One factor in the final fixing of the Jewish canon was the destruction of Jerusalem and the temple in AD 70. Separated from the temple worship, the Jews became more and more a people of the Book. The canonization of the Writings and the closing of the Jewish Bible is attributed to the Council of Jamnia dated around AD 90.

The Apocrypha. The Jewish Bible is the Christian Old Testament. For Protestant Christians, the Old Testament contains exactly the same material found in the Jewish Bible (arranged into thirty-nine books instead of the twenty-four in the Jewish Bible). Roman Catholic and Orthodox Christians, however, include in their Bibles several additional books termed "apocryphal" by Protestants and "deuterocanonical" (belonging to a second canon) by Roman Catholic and Orthodox Christians. These books were used by Jewish Christians who spoke Greek and included these writings in the Greek translation of the Hebrew Scriptures (the Septuagint).

Development of a New Testament Canon

The early Christians accorded to the Old Testament the same respect given it by the Jews. However, writing of their newfound life in Jesus Christ, Christians eventually developed a body of literature that became the New Testament.

The early authority of Christians. Although Christians accepted the Old Testament writings as sacred, a difference existed between Jewish and Christian attitudes toward the Old Testament. The presence of the Holy Spirit in the church and the fact of the resurrection made the writings of the Old Testament less primary for the early Christians. The Old Testament was a testimony to Christ and his gospel. In addition to the Old Testament, therefore, Christians accepted as authority the words of Jesus that were transmitted by word of mouth. Acts 20:35, for example, is an appeal to the sayings of Jesus. Paul, speaking to the elders of the Ephesian church, said, "'In all this I have given you an example that by such work we must support the weak, remembering the words of the Lord Jesus, for he himself said, 'It is more blessed to give than to receive.'" This saying is not recorded in our canonical Gospels.

Paul's letters. The letters of Paul were accepted as valuable enough to be preserved by the congregations to which they were sent. A collection of Paul's letters was made even before the writing of all the New Testament books. In 2 Peter 3:15 is a reference to letters from Paul: ". . . and regard the patience of our Lord as salvation. So also our beloved brother Paul wrote to you according to the wisdom given him, speaking of this as he does in all his letters. There are some things in them hard to understand, which the ignorant and unstable twist to their own destruction, as they do the other scriptures." Not only were the letters collected, but the statement that the letters of Paul were twisted by the ignorant and unstable just as "the other scriptures" indicates that they were considered authoritative on a par with the Old Testament.

The Gospels. By the mid-second century, Christians also regarded the Gospels as authoritative. They were written in the last half of the first century for specific purposes of instruction and edification. John 20:31 contains a general statement of purpose for that Gospel: ". . . these are written so that you may come to believe that Jesus is the Messiah, the Son of God, and that through believing you may have life in his name." The major purpose for which Christians wrote the Gospels was to proclaim Jesus Christ as Savior and Lord.

The document known as 2 Clement, dated in the mid-second century, is the earliest extant writing that recognized the Gospel material as being just as authoritative as the Old Testament writings. In one place the writer quotes words from Isaiah and then continues, "And again another scripture says, 'I came not to call the righteous, but sinners'" (2 Clement 4; Matt 9:13).

Completion of a New Testament Canon. One factor that influenced the churches to develop a definite New Testament canon was a list of canonical books organized by a heretic named Marcion who came to Rome from Pontus before AD 150. He had been brought up in orthodox circles, but under heretical influences he became convinced that the God of the Old Testament was inferior to the God of love made known in Jesus Christ. Therefore, Marcion rejected the Old Testament and formed a canon composed of the Gospel of Luke and ten letters of Paul.

Reacting to Marcion's heretical notions, the churches moved toward developing a definite canon. Before the close of the second century they were in general agreement upon the authority of the four Gospels, Acts, Paul's letters, and the general epistles (James; 1 and 2 Peter; 1, 2, and 3 John; and Jude). Certain other books now included in the New Testament were considered canonical among some Christians but not among others. Also, some books that were excluded, such as the Shepherd of Hermas, Barnabas, and 1 Clement, were considered authoritative in certain areas.

By the mid-fourth century Christian congregations were in general agreement upon the books to be included in the New Testament canon. Athanasius of Alexandria was the first Christian leader to list all twenty-seven books that compose the present New Testament, and only these twenty-seven, as belonging in the canon. In his thirty-ninth festal letter, written in 367, he listed the "books that are canonized and handed down to us believed to be divine." The list included the books that now appear in the Old and New Testaments.

In later years, various church councils further sanctioned the list. It should be noted, however, that the councils gave approval only after the Christian congregations had been led to use the twenty-seven books in the life and work of the church. The church did not use them simply because the councils gave them authority.

Chapter 10

The English Bible

From the mid-fourth century, when the church possessed the Scriptures in Hebrew and Greek, to the early seventeenth century, when the King James Version was published, many literary events took place. This most important English version of the Bible culminated a long and exciting background of attempts to make the Scriptures available in the languages of the rapidly spreading converts.

Early non-English Translations

Although the Old Testament was written mainly in Hebrew and the New Testament in Greek, the Bible was quickly translated into several other languages. The people of God were convinced that God's Word should not be confined only to those who spoke and read Hebrew or Greek.

The Old Testament was translated into Greek before the Christian era so that Greek-speaking Jews could have the Scriptures in their own language. Although Greek had become almost a second language in Italy as early as the second century BC and Paul wrote to the church in Rome in Greek, many people in the West used only Latin. A translation of the Bible into their native language, which was Latin, became necessary. In fact, the oldest Latin translations known to us are in the colloquial language of the relatively uneducated.

Latin translations also became necessary as the Christian faith spread to Africa, for Latin was the official language of that area. As the gospel spread to

Syria, a Syriac translation was necessary, and when the people in Egypt accepted the Christian faith, Egyptian versions were necessary.

These were useful early versions, and as the gospel spread still further, the Bible was translated into Armenian, Ethiopic, Georgian, and Arabic. The earliest translations into these particular languages were secondary translations from the Syriac. Nevertheless, the Latin translation of the Bible was the version that assumed increasing importance through the years; in the last part of the fourth century, Jerome, a leading Bible scholar, was commissioned by the Pope to revise the Old Latin Version in order to establish a standard translation. Although Jerome's work first met with misunderstanding and antagonism, it eventually became the Bible of the Roman Church. Jerome's translation is called the Vulgate, from the Latin word *vulgatus*, meaning "common," because it was a translation in the vernacular of the people.

Early English Translations

Many centuries had passed and the Christian faith had spread throughout much of the world before the Bible was translated into English—and for obvious reasons. The English-speaking Germanic tribes that had conquered the island of Britain in the fifth century were not converted in large numbers until the seventh century. Even then, several hundred years elapsed before English became a respectable written language, largely under the leadership of King Alfred the Great. At his urging, literate individuals at his court and in the monasteries began to translate many works from Latin into English. About one hundred years after his death in 901, there appeared the oldest surviving English version of the Bible, a portion of the Gospels. (The history of the English language is often divided into Old English or Anglo-Saxon, 450–1050; Middle English, 1040–1475; and Modern English, since 1475.)

Obviously, no English translation could be made before English-speaking peoples had heard the gospel. Christianity certainly came into the British Isles with Roman soldiers, and five British representatives attended a church council of the early fourth century. Not until 597, through the work of Augustine, a monk from the monastery of St. Andrew in Rome, did Christianity begin to prosper in England. Christianity grew rapidly, and within the next fifty years it was incorporated under the central authority of Rome. Still, there was no immediate attempt to translate the Bible into English after the labors of Augustine, for the majority of Christians could not read, and those who did used the Latin Bible.

During the Old English period a few efforts were made to make parts of the Bible known in the vernacular. Ordinary people learned parts of the Bible story in the form of poetry. Anglo-Saxon translations were inserted between the lines of the Latin text of Psalms, and some books of both the Old and the New Testaments were translated from the Latin Vulgate.

Wycliffe. Some of the books of the Bible were translated into Middle English, but the first English versions of the entire Bible were the work of John Wycliffe. His conviction was that all people, clergy or not, should be able to study the gospel in their own language. He declared that the Scriptures were the only law of the church and that church authority was not centered in the Pope and the cardinals. If this view were true, the Bible must be put into the language of the people.

Under the influence of Wycliffe, the entire Bible was translated from the Vulgate into English between 1380 and 1397. Two different versions were made in these years, and many copies of them produced, for even today one hundred and eighty manuscripts remain. Not only was the Bible translated into the language of the common people, but, just as important, it was also carried to the people by the "poor priests" who wandered two by two throughout the land.

Both Wycliffe versions are based on the Latin Vulgate and were copied and recopied by hand. There is a difference, however, in the two English translations. The earlier version is extremely literal; the Latin word order and construction are preserved even when they conflict with English idiom. For example, in 1 Samuel 2:10 the Latin has *Dominum formidabunt adversarii eius,* and in the earlier version that followed the Latin word order, this sentence was translated "The Lord shulen drede the adversaries of hym." This is poor theology and a worse translation. In the second version the translation was changed to good English, varying the Latin word order: "Adversaries of the Lord shulen drede hym." Throughout the translation of the Bible the later version is less literal and manifests a feeling for the native English idiom.

Tyndale. William Tyndale is remembered as the father of the King James Version and other authorized versions. For instead of making a secondary translation from the Latin Vulgate, he translated directly from the original Hebrew and Greek. This greatly influenced the translators who followed him. Also, because printing had been invented between the time of Wycliffe and Tyndale, the Tyndale translation was more widely circulated than the handwritten Wycliffe Bibles.

Tyndale shared with Wycliffe the "heretical" notion that the Bible should be read by people in their own language. As a young man he swore that if God spared his life he would make it possible for even the boy who drove the plow to know the Bible. The work of Tyndale happily coincided with that of several individuals who were to influence and assist him. One of these individuals was Erasmus, who provided a copy of the earliest printed Greek text, and Tyndale used Erasmus's Greek text in translating the New Testament into English. Martin Luther also provided help through his translation of the New Testament into German. Tyndale also consulted this translation.

Tyndale's translation of the New Testament was published in 1526. It was followed in 1530 by a translation of the first five books of the Old Testament (the Pentateuch) and in 1531 by the book of Jonah. In 1534 he added a revision of his New Testament, a revision of the Pentateuch, and further translations of the Old Testament. This translation from Joshua to Chronicles was not published until after his death.

Some understanding of Tyndale's work is important, for his work is reflected in the King James Version and the authorized versions following in the tradition of the King James Version. The work of Tyndale is based on the original languages. He used Erasmus's second and third editions of the Greek text for the New Testament and the Hebrew Old Testament of the Masoretes for the Old Testament. He also used the Vulgate and Luther's German translation, but he did not use the Wycliffe Bibles.

The translation was in free idiomatic English when compared with the Wycliffe versions. Although there is no relationship between the Tyndale version and earlier English translations, there is great similarity between the Tyndale Bible and the English translations that followed. It is estimated that one third of the actual wording of the King James Version comes from Tyndale, and it is obvious that the general structure of the King James and other authorized versions comes from the work of Tyndale. Some scholars have even said that "ninety per cent of Tyndale is reproduced in the King James Version of the New Testament."[1]

Notice the similarity between the beginning of 1 Corinthians 13 by Tyndale and the King James Version:

> Though I spake with the tonges of men and angels, and yet had no love, I were even as sounding brasse: or as a tynklynge Cymball. And though I coulde prophesy, and vnderstode all secrets, and all knowledge: yee, yf I had all fayth so that I coulde move mountayns oute of ther places, and yet had no love, I were nothynge. And though I bestowed all my gooddes to fede the poore, and though I gave my body even that I burned, and yet had no love, it profeteth me nothinge. Love suffreth longe, and is corteous. Love envieth not. (Tyndale)

> Though I speak with the tongues of men and of angels, and have not charity, I am become as sounding brass, or a tinkling cymbal. And though I have *the gift of prophecy*, and understand all mysteries, and all knowledge; and though I have all faith, so that I could remove mountains, and have not charity, I am nothing. And

though I bestow all my goods to feed *the poor*, and though I give my body to be burned, and have not charity, it profiteth me nothing. Charity suffereth long, *and* is kind; charity envieth not. (KJV)

Other pre-King James English translations. Between the work of Tyndale and the publication of the King James Version of the Bible, a variety of translators' efforts appeared. In order came the Coverdale Bible, Matthew's Bible, the Great Bible, the Geneva Bible, and the Bishops' Bible.

The Coverdale Bible (1535) was the first complete English Bible *printed*. It was the work of Myles Coverdale, a graduate of Cambridge who had left the Augustinian order after being influenced by the Reformation movement. The title of his work (*Biblia, The Bible, that is, the holy Scripture of the Olde and New Testament, faithfully and truly translated out of Douche and Latyn in to Englische*) indicates that it was a secondary translation out of German and Latin instead of a direct translation from the Hebrew and Greek.

Matthew's Bible was published in 1537. Thomas Matthew is the pen name for John Rogers, a former associate of Tyndale. His Bible is basically the work of Tyndale—his New Testament and as much of the Old Testament as Tyndale had translated. The remainder of the Old Testament and the Apocrypha are basically the translation of Coverdale.

The same year that Matthew's Bible was published and licensed by the king, a new edition of Coverdale's Bible was published, issued "with the king's license." To have two widely variant translations circulating under royal authority was confusing. To correct this, Thomas Cromwell asked Coverdale to revise the Matthews Bible so that it could become the standard and take the place of the two Bibles then competing for authority. Coverdale complied with the request, and the Great Bible became the authorized Bible. It was called "great" because the pages of the 1539 edition measured 16 1/2 by 11 inches.

The Geneva Bible grew out of renewed persecution of Protestants in England. The work of Coverdale and Rogers took place in the latter years of the reign of Henry VIII who had broken with the Pope and supported the Church of England. Edward VI, the son and successor of Henry VIII, maintained this position, but in 1553, Mary came to the throne and tried to move England back into the Roman Catholic Church. Utterly immoderate in her zeal, she caused those who refused to return to the Roman church to be burned at the stake as heretics. She was called "Bloody Mary" because of this persecution, and many Protestants fled from England.

One group of Protestants went to Geneva, Switzerland, where they engaged in Bible translation and published the Geneva Bible in April of 1560. By the time of its publication, Queen Elizabeth had become the reigning monarch in England, so the Bible was dedicated to her with admonitions to "root out and cut down these weeds and impediments [the Catholic adherents to the Pope]." The title of the Geneva Bible indicated that it was translated from the Hebrew and Greek and that various previous translations were consulted. The Geneva Bible was the one used by the Pilgrim fathers.

The immediate predecessor of the King James Version was the Bishops' Bible, which resulted from reaction to the Geneva Bible. The bishops and other clergymen in England had no part in making the Geneva Bible. This lack of relationship between the English clergy and the Geneva translators, along with the outspoken Calvinism expressed in its notes, made the Geneva Bible unsuitable for church use in England. However, the widespread use of the Geneva Bible highlighted the deficiencies of the Great Bible, and in 1561 Archbishop Matthew Parker submitted a proposal that the Great Bible be revised. This would provide an official translation to rank with the offensive Geneva Bible. The work of revision was completed in seven years, and on 22 September 1568 copies of the Bishops' Bible were sent to the Queen.

The revisers used the Great Bible as the basis of their work and departed from it where translation did not accurately represent the original. They compared other translations and added no bitter annotations to the text. By the close of the sixteenth century, then, several competent translations of the Bible had been made in England. These early works have been important to the later translations of the Bible and are a valuable part of the rich Christian heritage of all English-speaking people today.

The Roman Catholics in England, influenced by the Protestant translations of the Bible into English, provided an English translation for themselves called the Rheims and Douai Version. The name results from the fact that the New Testament was published in 1582 by the English College in Rheims, France. The Old Testament was published in 1609–1610 in Douai by the English college that had moved there from Rheims. This Bible was a translation from the Vulgate, and for the New Testament the Greek text was also consulted. It was accompanied by a commentary that gave the reader the proper Roman Catholic interpretation. This version was revised in 1750 and was made the approved English version for Catholics in America in 1810.

Note

[1] Herbert Gordon May, *Our English Bible in the Making* (Philadelphia: The Westminster Press, 1952), 26.

Chapter 11

The King James Version

The Bible translation best known to us is not that of Wycliffe or Tyndale. It is not even the Great Bible, the Geneva Bible, or the Bishops' Bible. It is the King James Version. The King James Version has become *the* Bible to many people. That it too grew out of specific needs and drew upon previous works is not always recognized.

The Need for Another Version

When Queen Elizabeth died in 1603, James I became the king of England. During his journey from Scotland to England an event occurred that ultimately led to the version of the Bible bearing his name. He was presented with a "millenary petition" containing about 800 signatures and a list of grievances from Puritan clergy.

The king invited the clergy who signed the petition to a conference that met at Hampton Court in 1604. The conference failed to accomplish the aims of the Puritans. In fact, at the conference James threatened to force out of the land all who did not conform to the established church, and from that day onward the Puritans were to be considered the foes of King James.

However, a proposal by one Puritan was given warm support by the king. The Puritan was President John Reynolds of Corpus Christi College at Oxford, and his proposal was that there be a new translation of the Bible because the ones produced in the reigns of Henry VIII and Edward VI were "corrupt and not answerable to the truth of the original."

Plans and Process

The resolution that passed in the Hampton Court Conference was "That a translation be made of the whole Bible, as consonant as can be to the original Hebrew and Greek; and this to be set out and printed, without any marginal notes, and only to be used in all Churches of England in time of divine service." King James approved the resolution, declaring that he had never yet seen a Bible "well translated in English." He continued, "I wish some special pains were taken for a uniform translation, which should be done by the best-learned men in both Universities, then reviewed by the Bishops, presented to the Privy Council, lastly ratified by Royal authority, to be read in the whole Church, and none other."

Individuals were appointed for the work of translation, and they were organized into six companies, two companies each at Westminster, Cambridge, and Oxford. Three companies would translate the Old Testament, two the New Testament, and one the Apocrypha. They received general directions concerning their work.[1]

- Follow the Bishops' Bible and devise a text "as little altered as the truth of the original will permit."
- Maintain forms of biblical names as nearly as possible in the way that they are commonly used.
- Keep the old ecclesiastical words—"church" instead of "congregation," for example.
- Leave chapter divisions unaltered, if possible, and do not add marginal notes except to clarify the meaning of Hebrew or Greek words that could not be explained in the text. Cross-references can be added in the margin, however.

Each person in a company was to take a section of the Scriptures and translate it independently. Then the entire company would come together and agree upon a standard translation. When a company completed a book, they sent it to the other translators for their consideration and suggestions. Clergy throughout the land were involved in the project by making it known that a translation was underway and by inviting suggestions from those interested.

Some translations earlier than the Bishops' Bible were mentioned specifically in the directions. They were those of Tyndale, Matthew (Rogers), Coverdale, Whitechurch,[2] and the Geneva Bible. These translations were to be used when they agreed better with the original text than the Bishops' Bible. When all the companies completed their task, the entire work was to be reviewed by a group of twelve individuals (two from each company) before it was sent to the printer.

In an introduction for the readers, the translators indicated that they had followed these plans generally.

> Truly (good Christian Reader) we never thought from the beginning, that we should need to make a new translation, nor yet to make of a bad one a good one . . . but to make a good one better, or out of many good ones, one principal good one, not justly to be excepted against; that hath been our endeavour, that our mark.[3]

The translators declared that they did not neglect consulting

> the translators or commentators, Chaldee, Hebrew, Syrian, Greek, or Latin, no nor the Spanish, French, Italian, or Dutch; neither did we disdain to revise that which we had done, and to bring back to the anvil that which we had hammered: but having and used as great helps as were needful, and fearing no reproach for slowness, nor coveting praise for expedition, we have at the length, through the good hand of the Lord upon us, brought the work to that pass that you see.[4]

The introduction indicated that an alternate translation was put in the margin where a great probability indicated such a reading. For example, many words are found in the Scriptures only once, and many rare names of birds, beasts, stones, and other objects are found. "Now in such a case, doth not a margin do well to admonish the Reader to seek further, and not to conclude or dogmatize upon this or that peremptorily?"[5]

The translators point out that the same word is often translated in several different ways. "Another thing we think good to admonish thee of (gentle Reader) that we have not tied our selves to an uniformity of phrasing, or to an identity of words, as some peradventrue would wish that we had done, because they observe, that some learned men somewhere, have been as exact as they could that way."[6] Still, they continue to say that they have "avoided the scrupulosity of the Puritans, who leave the old ecclesiastical words, and betake them to other, as when they put *washing* for *baptism*, and *congregation* instead of *church*."[7]

Early Reception

The translators themselves were not sure that the people would welcome their translation. In fact, there was good reason to believe that the translation would be condemned. In the very first paragraph of their introduction, the laborers said,

Zeal to promote the common good, whether it be by devising any thing ourselves, or revising that which hath been laboured by others, deserveth certainly much respect and esteem, but yet findeth but cold entertainment in the world. It is welcomed with suspicion, instead of love, and with emulation instead of thanks: and if there be any hole for cavil to enter, (and cavil, if it do not find an hole, will make one) it is sure to be misconstrued and in danger to be condemned.[8]

Perhaps the most forthright criticism of the new translation came from Hugh Broughton. Broughton was a distinguished scholar described by the English Hebraist John Lightfoot as a man "renowned in many Nations for Rare Skill in Salems and Athens Tongues and Familiar Acquaintance with all Rabbinical Learning." Upon looking at the new work, Broughton declared that it bred in him "a sadness that will grieve me while I breathe, it is so ill done. Tell His Majesty that I had rather be rent in pieces with wild horses, than any such translation by my consent should be urged upon poor churches . . . . The new edition crosseth me. I require it to be burnt."[9]

It has been suggested that Broughton resented the fact that he was not invited to serve as one of the translators. Broughton himself had been preparing a translation based on the Geneva Bible and felt that the Geneva Bible was the best English version in existence. On the other hand, he had nothing good to say for the Bishops' Bible, the translation on which the King James Version was based.[10]

Although the translators were fearful and Broughton condemned it, three editions appeared in quick succession in the very year of publication.

Later History of the King James Version

That the King James Version, like the earlier versions, has undergone a series of revisions is not so well known. As early as 1613 an edition appeared that had over 300 variations from the 1611 edition. The Cambridge edition of 1629 was carefully revised, and an edition of 1638 seriously attempted to correct some of the readings.

A bill was brought before the Parliament in 1653 that resulted in the appointment of a committee to revise the King James Version if it should be found necessary. The project was not undertaken at that time, but an extensive revision was published in 1762. Seven years later another edition was published that included modernization of spelling and punctuation and correction of various errors. The 1769 edition represents the KJV as it is known today.

Notes

[1] Fifteen specific rules were given. They are summarized here from the list in Brooke Foss Westcott's *A General View of the History of the English Bible*, 3rd ed. rev., by William Aldis Wright (New York: The Macmillan Co., 1922), 114-16.

[2] The Great Bible was called Whitechurch's because he was the publisher of the fifth edition.

[3] "The Translators to the Reader," *The Reader's Bible* (New York: Oxford University Press, 1951), pxxvi.

[4] Ibid., xxviii.

[5] Ibid.

[6] Ibid., xxix.

[7] Ibid., xxx.

[8] Ibid., xi.

[9] Cited in F. F. Bruce, *The English Bible: A History of Translations* (London: Lutterworth, 1961), 107.

[10] Ibid., 106-107.

Chapter 12

Modern Versions to the Revised Standard Version

The King James Version of the Bible grew out of specific needs of seventeenth-century English Christians. It has served well the English-speaking Christian world. However, just as previous translations led to the production of the King James Version, so the King James Version has served as a guide and basis for still further translations. This chapter will discuss both the works that have continued in the tradition of the King James Version and the more independent translations up through the mid-twentieth century.

Developments since the King James Version

Three major developments following the appearance of the King James Version made new translations necessary. Scholars determined more accurately what the biblical writers originally wrote; knowledge of biblical languages, especially the Greek of the New Testament, increased; and the English language underwent considerable change and development. This last factor is probably the most compelling.

Textual studies. The Old Testament was written mainly in Hebrew. Jewish scholars copied the Hebrew manuscripts by hand with extraordinary care, having the objective that there would be no variation between the original copy and the new copy. Once a copy was made, the original was discarded. By this practice a standard text without variations in numerous manuscripts was achieved. Thus, when later translators approach the Old Testament, they have a standard text that has been passed down by the

Jewish scholars. It is called the Masoretic Text, for it was copied and edited by Jewish scholars called the "Masoretes" who made notations concerning the Hebrew Bible. Until recently the earliest copy of the Old Testament text was a tenth century AD Masoretic manuscript (the Codex Leningrad in the Russian National Library in St. Petersburg [at one time called Leningrad]).

Old Testament textual discoveries since the translation of the King James Version, therefore, play a relatively small part in the need for new translations. However, some materials have been uncovered that aid the translator of the Old Testament. In 1890 a number of biblical fragments were discovered in a Cairo genizah—a storeroom in which Jews placed sacred texts no longer fit for use. The Cairo genizah yielded about a quarter of a million biblical, liturgical, and other fragments chiefly in Hebrew, Aramaic, Arabic, Samaritan, and Greek. The Dead Sea Scrolls also contain biblical material that has aided in textual study of the Old Testament. Especially important are scrolls of Isaiah dated nearly one thousand years earlier than manuscripts previously known. Old Testament textual discoveries confirm that Jewish scribes copied the Hebrew Bible with care. The copies of the Old Testament books contain much less variation than ancient copies of New Testament books.

Textual discoveries have played an important part in recent translations of the New Testament. The text used by the translators of the New Testament in the time of King James was basically the text of Erasmus that was produced hurriedly at the instigation of a printer at Basle. It was based on available manuscripts that were neither the most ancient nor the most valuable. The Erasmus text was criticized almost from the beginning of its use. Because it was the earliest printed text, however, it was standard for 200 years and used in producing the King James Version. Not until the middle of the nineteenth century was work begun that resulted in a new standard text. New manuscripts were discovered. Two of the earliest and best were "Vaticanus" and "Sinaiticus."

On the basis of new textual discoveries, scholars developed a more acceptable theory by which to produce a more correct text. B. F. Westcott and F. J. A. Hort in 1881 printed a Greek text with an elaborate introduction and notes on special passages. Their work has formed the basis for all later textual criticism of the Greek New Testament. These nineteenth-century works were available for the translations made in the last part of the nineteenth and the first part of the twentieth centuries.

Since the beginning of the twentieth century, additional work has been done in textual studies. About 4,500 witnesses to the Greek text of the New Testament are known today. Advances in textual criticism have also been made in the use of ancient lectionaries, versions, and quotations of the New Testament in the Church Fathers.

The major result of these advances was expressed by Floyd V. Filson in 1951:

> As a result of these and similar discoveries it has become increasingly clear that no future finds will alter in any essential the text of our Greek Testament. There are indeed numerous minor variations between manuscripts, and scholars weigh them carefully. But these are relatively unimportant. Even in 1882, as Hort then said, we had a substantially reliable text, and the discoveries of third-century and even second-century evidence make it doubly certain that we know in all essentials what the first-century writers said.[1]

Greek Grammar. Many people are surprised to learn that scholars have discovered only recently the nature of the Greek in which the New Testament was written. Although agreement on the precise nature of New Testament Greek is not yet universal, it is generally agreed that the Greek of the New Testament was basically the nonliterary, or vernacular, Greek.

The great advance in the field of New Testament Greek grammar was mainly the result of the papyri discoveries in Egypt. As the papyri from Egypt were published, the "problem" of New Testament Greek was soon seen as not so much of a problem. Adolf Deissmann is credited with the discovery and early work in this area. Such grammarians as the Baptist scholar A. T. Robertson quickly applied the discovery to the area of New Testament Greek grammar, and these studies have greatly influenced translators.

English. A comparison of previous selections cited from early translations shows that the English of the sixteenth and seventeenth centuries is quite different from the English of the twentieth and twenty-first centuries. One most obvious difference is the use of pronouns. The King James Version regularly uses "thou," "thee," "thy," "thine," and "ye." These forms are obsolete and have no place in a modern English translation.

Along with these archaic pronouns are archaic verb forms. The King James Version uses many personal endings that have gone out of use except for rare cases, as in poetic and devotional language. We do not use "hast." Readers acquainted only with modern English would have trouble with terms like "doth," "quoth," durst," "wot not," "trow," and "me thinks."

Perhaps the development in English *demanding* a revision, or new translation, is the modification or change in the meanings of words. An interesting example of a change in meaning is the word "prevent," occurring in both the Old and New Testaments. In the sixteenth and seventeenth centuries, "prevent" meant "to go before." The psalmist in Psalm 119:147 declares that he "prevented the dawning of the morning" (KJV). He got up before dawn. (See also Matt 17:25 and 1 Thess 4:15.) Today the word expresses almost exclusively the idea of "hindering." The translators of the Revised Standard Version point out that there are more than 300 English words used in the King James Version in a sense substantially different from the way they are used today.

Authorized Versions Since 1611

The first Bible "appointed to be read in churches" in England was the Great Bible of 1539. The second was the Bishops' Bible of 1568. The King James Version is really only the third "authorized" English version. (It was authorized by the king before the work of translation.) Since its appearance several other versions have been authorized, at least in the sense that a competent group gave approval to the undertaking and representative and responsible committees completed the work of translation. The English Revised Version of 1881–1885 was the first authorized version of the Bible after the King James Version. In 1901 the American Standard Version, a variant of the English Revised Version, was published for American readers. In 1946–1952 the Revised Standard Version of the Bible was published by a group of American scholars, and in 1961–1970 the New English Bible was published in Great Britain.

The English Revised Version. The English Revised Version of 1881–1885 was a revision of the King James Version. Parallel to and following the developments in biblical studies discussed earlier came demands in England for a new revision of the New Testament. On 10 February 1870, a resolution was made in the Upper House of the Convocation of Canterbury that a study be made as to the desirability of revising the Authorized Version of the New Testament (later amended to include the Old Testament).

The committee appointed to determine the need for a revision presented its report on 3 May 1870. The report, adopted by both houses of Convocation, declared that it was "desirable that a revision of the Authorized Version of the Holy Scriptures be undertaken." It was clearly understood that the work was to be a revision. "We do not contemplate any new translation of the Bible, or any alteration of the language, except where in the judgment of the most competent scholars such change is necessary."[2] It was declared that the language style of the King James Version should be closely followed and that the revision should include both marginal readings and changes that may be found necessary to insert in the text of the King James Version.

Although the revision was basically the work of Englishmen, an American committee was organized to assist in the task of translation. The preface to the New Testament section tells of the work of the Americans.

> We [the English revisers] transmitted to them from time to time each several portions of our First Revision, and received from them in return their criticisms and suggestions. These we considered with much care and attention during the time we were engaged on our Second Revision. We then sent over to them the various portions of the Second Revision as they were completed, and received further suggestions, which, like the former, were closely and carefully considered. Last of all, we forwarded to them the Revised Version in its final form; and a list of those passages in which they desired to place on record their preference of other readings and renderings will be found at the end of the volume.[3]

The New Testament was published ten and one-half years after the work had begun, and the Old Testament was completed in fourteen years. Old Testament scholars generally agree that the translation of the Old Testament was a creditable job. Like the 1611 translators, the revisers used the Masoretic Hebrew text as the basis for their work; but, having a clearer understanding of the Hebrew text than the earlier scholars did, they rendered the Hebrew into better English.

The work of the New Testament translators was based upon the achievements of the nineteenth-century textual critics. In fact, the most distinguished textual critics in England were invited to join the work. While it progressed, B. F. Westcott and F. J. A. Hort labored on their Greek text of the New Testament. Since they worked with the committee, their textual labors were placed at the disposal of their colleagues. Thus, the Revised Version of the New Testament was a great advance over the King James Version, insofar as the Greek text is concerned.

The English of the Revised Version is more open to criticism. Perhaps the rules followed by the revisers account for the Revised Version often being called a "schoolmaster's translation." The preface affirms that the revisers did not consider that their duty was to conform the language of the Revised Version to current usage. Referring to the use of words not found in the King James and earlier versions, they said, "We have usually satisfied ourselves that such words were employed by standard writers of nearly the same date."[4] It is obvious that the revisers consciously aimed at being both Elizabethan and understandable. As a result of such limitation, the Revised Version is as literal a translation as could be made without being impossible to read as English. The Revised Version, therefore, did not solve all problems. That is, it did not bring an end to translations.

The American Standard Version. The American Standard Version of 1901 grew out of the work of the American scholars who assisted in the English Revised Version. The American committee was organized in 1871 and began its work in October of 1872. Its task was to review the revisions of the British committee and to make suggestions. In 1875 the British committee agreed that they would consider the suggestions of the Americans and that the American committee would be allowed to present in an appendix to the Revised Version their conclusions that were not accepted and used in the English Revised Version. This appendix would contain all of the important differences that the British declined to adopt.

This appendix was to be published in the Revised Version for fourteen years, and the American committee pledged that for the fourteen years it would neither publish nor sanction publication of any edition of the work other than that issued by the British committee. After publication of the English Revised Version, the American committee continued its work because it saw that an "American recension" of the Revised Version might be needed.[5]

In accord with the agreement not to issue an American edition for at least fourteen years after the English edition, the American Version was not published until August of 1901. The preparation of the new edition was more than merely the "mechanical work of transferring the readings of the Appendix to the text." The American scholars declared that as a result of a lack of further connection with the British revisers, they "have felt themselves to be free to go beyond the task of incorporating the Appendix in the text; and are no longer restrained from introducing into the text a large number of those suppressed emendations."[6]

The Revised Standard Version. The English Revised Version and the American Standard Version have been described as "premature" revisions. They were undertaken before the revolutionary discoveries of the first half of the twentieth century. Of course, it was not possible for the scholars to foresee the premature nature of their venture.

Textual discoveries and the theory based on them have advanced. Ernest Cadman Colwell, an American textual critic, finds that 1925 is the approximate date when a change took place in textual theory and practice. It consisted of a modification of the theory and practice of Westcott and Hort. The change, though not radical, was important.

In the years immediately following the discovery of the significance of the papyri, a high point was reached in the study of Greek grammar. In 1906 J. H. Moulton published the first volume of his New Testament Greek grammar. In 1914 A. T. Robertson published his massive grammar. In 1929 the second volume of Moulton's work, completed by W. R. Howard, was published. (In 1963 the third and final volume of Moulton's work was published by Nigel Turner.)

According to Luther Weigle, the major defect of the English Revised and the American Standard versions is that these are "literal, word-for-word translations, which follow the order of the Greek words, so far as this is possible, rather than the order which is natural to English."[7] He declared also that "in the Bible we have not merely an historical document and a classic of English literature, but the Word of God . . . . That Word must not be hidden in ancient phrases which have changed or lost their meaning; it must stand forth in language that is direct and clear and meaningful to the people of today."[8]

In 1937 the International Council of Religious Education authorized a revision of the American Standard Version. The directive was that the resulting version should "embody the best results of modern scholarship as to the meaning of the Scriptures, and express this meaning in English diction which is designed for use in public and private worship and preserves those qualities which have given to the King James Version a supreme place in English literature."[9] The Revised Standard Version of the New Testament was published in 1946, and in 1952 the Revised Standard Version of the Bible, containing the Old and the New Testaments, was published.

The Revised Standard Version is not a "wooden" translation as were the Revised Version and the American Standard Version. Yet it remained a revision and not a new translation into the vernacular of the twentieth century. Such a fresh translation was achieved in Great Britain.

The New English Bible. The same developments in biblical studies that influenced American scholars to revise the American Standard Version and to produce the Revised Standard Version of the Bible led scholars in Great Britain to see the need for a new translation of the English Bible used in the British Isles. In May 1946, the General Assembly of the Church of Scotland received a recommendation that a translation of the Bible be made "in the language of the present day." In October, delegates from the Church of England, the Church of Scotland, the Methodist, Baptist, and Congregationalist churches met and recommended that a translation be made. At the very outset a decision was reached: "what was now needed was not another revision of the Authorized Version but a genuinely new translation, in which an attempt should be made consistently to use the idiom of contemporary English."[10]

In 1961 the New Testament section of the New English Bible was published and in 1970 the entire Bible was published. The translators discussed their procedure in an introduction: "We have conceived our task to be that of understanding the original as precisely as we could (using all available aids), and then saying again in our own native idiom what we believed the author to be saying in his."[11]

The translators declared that they intended to offer a translation in the strict sense and not a paraphrase; they did not wish to encroach on the work of the commentator. "Taken as a whole, our version claims to be a translation, free, it may be, rather than literal, but a faithful translation nevertheless, so far as we could compass it."[12]

The translators saw themselves as producing a work that would be used in the churches as the King James Version was used. The language has a certain style and is formal enough to be used in public worship. The translation, however, was outside the King James tradition. The method of translation was a thought-for-thought translation rather than a word-for-word translation. The principle followed in such a translation is now called the principle of dynamic or functional equivalence and will be seen in the majority of the private translations in the first half of the twentieth century.

Private Translations

During the twentieth century a multitude of private translations were published. The works of James Moffatt, Edgar Goodspeed, Helen Barrett Montgomery, and J. B. Phillips will illustrate the task and result of modern private translations in the first part of the twentieth century.

James Moffatt was an able Scottish scholar who taught in Scotland and later at Union Theological Seminary in the United States. His outstanding contribution to biblical translation began as early as 1901. That year he published *The Historical New Testament*, based on a critical Greek text by D. Eberhard Nestle. *The Historical New Testament* was Moffatt's translation of the New Testament books arranged in chronological order and containing an introduction, historical tables, critical notes, and an appendix.

The translation that made Moffatt famous, *The New Testament: A New Translation*, issued in 1913, is different from the work of 1901. This 1913 New Testament translation is based on the critical Greek text of H. von Soden, and the books are arranged in the usual order. Moffatt attempted to translate the New Testament exactly as one would translate any piece of contemporary Greek prose.

In 1924 Moffatt published a new translation of the Old Testament, declaring it to be a fresh translation from the original Hebrew. A one-volume edition of the entire Bible was published in 1926 as *A New Translation of the Bible*.

Edgar J. Goodspeed of the University of Chicago published a translation of the New Testament in 1923. His preparation for the task had begun as early as 1887 when he initiated a study of the Gospel of John with the Greek text of Westcott and Hort. Later, for twenty years, he taught the Greek New Testament to university students.

However, the actual task of translating the New Testament for publication began almost as an accident. At a regular meeting of the New Testament Club at the University of Chicago on 24 February 1920, Dr. Goodspeed read a paper on modern speech translations. His criticism of some of the translations led one of his colleagues to remark that Goodspeed should make a translation of his own. This brought forth laughter at the expense of Dr. Goodspeed, but a representative of the University of Chicago Press was present and took the suggestion seriously. Shortly the University of Chicago Press invited Dr. Goodspeed to undertake a translation for publication.

Before the actual publication of the work, newspaper reporters heard of the translation and publicized it widely in articles and editorials. When the actual translation was published, many people protested the changes from the King James Version and called the translation "journalistic" and "newspaper English." Of course, Goodspeed simply pointed out that the Greek New Testament was written not in a fine literary style but in the "common" Greek. It was the language of the laborers, the tradesmen, the slaves—not the polished language of the elite.

The work of Goodspeed is known to many because it is included in *The Complete Bible: An American Translation* that was published in 1939. This was the work of a group of translators who attempted to put the Old Testament as well as the New Testament into the American language in the sense that the writings of Lincoln, Roosevelt, and Wilson are American. In addition to his translation of the New Testament, Goodspeed contributed a translation of the Apocrypha for *The Complete Bible.*

In 1924, the year after Goodspeed's New Testament translation, Helen Barrett Montgomery published a translation of the New Testament titled *The Centenary Translation of the New Testament*. It was called the "centenary" translation because it commemorated the completion of the first hundred years of work of the American Baptist Publication Society. The lack of attention to Montgomery's translation was doubtless due to the fact that Goodspeed published his translation only a year before and received wide attention—and to the fact that Montgomery was a woman. Montgomery's work, however, maintains an important position in the history of Bible translation. Montgomery was an 1884 graduate of Wellesley College where she earned an undergraduate degree in Greek. After graduation from college, she was involved with the church and the church's mission program, becoming a licensed minister in 1892, publishing eight books on missions, and serving two terms as president of what was then the Northern Baptist Convention. She also involved herself in the Woman's Suffrage Movement and other social and educational reform movements. With Susan B. Anthony she founded the Woman's Educational and Industrial Union of Rochester, New York (WEIU), and served as first president of the organization.

An immediate context for Montgomery's translation was her Bible teaching at her church. In a note on "Translating the New Testament" after the publication of the Centenary Translation, Montgomery spoke of one of her first ventures in ministry—a Bible class for underprivileged boys. In that class Montgomery found that the "stately and old expressions which had such a charm for the literary-minded, were a bar and a hindrance to the less educated."Her aim, then, in making her own translation was "to consider young people, busy Sunday school teachers, and foreigners, and to try to make it plain."[13]

In the introduction to the translation, Montgomery specified that her translation was "chiefly designed for the ordinary reader." It was "intended to remove the veil that a literary or formal translation inevitably puts between the reader of only average education and the meaning of the text." Four specific aims are listed that are designed to carry out that goal:

(1) To offer a translation in the language of everyday life, that does not depart too much from the translations already familiar and beloved.
(2) To retain the customary division into chapters, even though this is not justified on grounds of strict scholarship; and still further to name the chapters, as an aid to remembering the contents of each book.
(3) To provide paragraph headings as an aid to finding a desired passage, and as a further help in memorizing the events as they are recorded.
(4) To use every aid of typography to indicate dialogue, quotation, and other elements of the narrative.[14]

Nowhere does Montgomery indicate that her translation is designed especially for women—even though in an announcement of its publication, the American Baptist Publication Society said of the translation, "Mrs. Montgomery has given a sweet, womanly touch to the finer passages."[15] Indeed, when a contemporary reader moves to the Centenary New Testament from translations such as the New Revised Standard Version, the reader is impressed with the lack of what we today call inclusive language. Montgomery's use of the masculine pronoun as a common pronoun follows traditional usage, for example. Montgomery's translation of 1 Corinthians 2:1, 11, 13-15 reads:

And when I came to you, brothers, I came not to proclaim God's great secret purpose in fine language or philosophy . . . .

For what man knows the depths of man except the man's own inner spirit? Even so, also, the Spirit of God knows the deeps profound of God . . . . Of these high themes we speak in words not taught by human philosophy, but by the Spirit; interpreting spiritual things to spiritual men. The unspiritual man rejects the teachings of God's Spirit; for to him it is folly. He cannot understand it, for it is spiritually discerned. But the spiritual man discerns everything, yet is himself discerned by no one.

The New Revised Standard Version uses inclusive language:

When I came to you, brothers and sisters, I did not come proclaiming the mystery of God to you in lofty words or wisdom. . . . For what human being knows what is truly human except the human spirit that is within? So also no one comprehends what is truly God's except the Spirit of God. . . . And we speak of these things in words not taught by human wisdom but taught by the Spirit, interpreting spiritual things to those who are spiritual.

Those who are unspiritual do not receive the gifts of God's Spirit, for they are foolishness to them, and they are unable to understand them because they are spiritually discerned. Those who are spiritual discern all things, and they are themselves subject to no one else's scrutiny.

Montgomery's translation does contain passages that reveal a definite feminist interest. Roger A. Bullard discusses five exemplary passages.[16] Many contemporary translations parallel Montgomery's treatment of four specific passages (described below). The fifth passage is 1 Timothy 2:15, a difficult passage indicating that in spite of the fact that Eve was the first to sin, women can still attain salvation—by bearing children. Montgomery translates this: "Notwithstanding she will be saved by the Child-bearing; (so will they all), if they continue in faith and love . . . ." This makes the verse refer to a woman's bearing of the child Jesus. Montgomery makes this clear by capitalizing the word "child" and adding to the text "(so shall they all)," making it clear that men receive salvation in the same way. (The RSV and NRSV contain the following note: "This much debated verse has also been translated (a) 'she will be saved through the birth of the Child' [referring to Jesus Christ], or (b) 'she will be brought safely through childbirth.'")

The four passages with translations followed by many contemporary translators are Romans 16:1 (describing Phoebe as "a minister [*diakonos*] of the church at Cenchreae" and adding a footnote referring to the use of the word *diakonos* at

1 Cor 3:5, 1 Tim 4:6, Eph 3:7, and 1 Thess 3:2); 1 Timothy 3:11 (describing the "women" referred to in the passage as "deaconesses"); Romans 16:7 (referring to "Andronicus and Junia [a woman] . . . who are notable among the apostles" instead of "Andronicus and Junias" [a man]); and 1 Corinthians 14:34-36 (placing the statement denying women the right to speak in church on the lips of Paul's opponents instead of on the lips of Paul).

First Corinthians 14:34-36 is treated as the voice of opponents whose views or words Paul quotes in order immediately to refute or qualify them:

"In your congregation" [you write], "as in all the churches of the saints, let the women keep silence in the churches, for they are not permitted to speak. On the contrary, let them be subordinate, as also says the law. And if they want to learn anything, let them ask their own husbands at home, for it is shameful for a woman to speak in church." What, was it from you that the word of God went forth, or to you only did it come?

This results in a condemnation of those who are forbidding the women to speak! This is not a whim of Montgomery. In numerous other places in the Corinthian letters and three places in Galatians, Montgomery identifies quotations from real or imagined opponents of Paul.[17] Sharyn Dowd has studied Montgomery's interpretation of 1 Corinthians 14:34-35 as a Corinthian slogan that Paul rejects and she has concluded that Montgomery probably came to this interpretation through the work of Katharine C. Bushnell, a medical missionary to China who, upon her return to this country, produced a Bible correspondence course in which she analyzed passages dealing with the status of women. Dowd suggests that Montgomery was influenced by Bushnell's publication titled *God's Word to Women: One Hundred Bible Studies on Woman's Place in the Divine Economy* (Piedmont CA: self published, n.d.). Montgomery published a review of this book for a Baptist publication in 1924. She praised Bushnell for showing that "both Paul and the Bible in general when properly translated and understood favor the widest possible service of women."[18]

In part, the work of Montgomery probably received less attention than deserved because she chose to frame her translation more in line with the King James tradition than did Moffatt and Goodspeed. The translation of J. B. Phillips is at the very opposite pole in the spectrum from literal (formal equivalence) to free (functional equivalence). J. B. Phillips, who has become well known as a translator of the New Testament, was a pastor who began this translation during the Second World War in an effort to assist members of his congregation to understand the message of the Bible and to relieve the weariness of wartime civilian duties. His first publication was *Letters to Young Churches* (1947), a translation of the letters of Paul. F. F. Bruce declared in 1961 that "undoubtedly, of all modern English translations of the New Testament epistles, this is one of the best—perhaps actually the best—for the ordinary reader."[19]

When compared with the work of Montgomery, and even Moffatt and Goodspeed, the work of Phillips is seen to be more a paraphrase than a translation. It attempts to give the meaning of the writer rather than the English equivalent of the Greek words. Compare Phillips's treatment of 1 Corinthians 2:1, 11, 13-15 with that of Montgomery and the NRSV cited earlier (but note the lack of inclusive language):

> In the same way, my brothers, when I came to proclaim to you God's secret purpose, I did not come equipped with any brilliance of speech or intellect . . .
> . . . For who could really understand a man's inmost thoughts except the spirit of the man himself? . . .
> It is these things that we talk about, not using the expressions of the human intellect but those which the Holy Spirit teaches us, explaining spiritual things to those who are spiritual.
> But the unspiritual man simply cannot accept the matters which the Spirit deals with—they just don't make sense to him, for, after all, you must be spiritual to see spiritual things.

In addition to the epistles, J. B. Phillips also translated the Gospels (1952), the book of Acts (1955), and the book of Revelation (1957). In 1958 a one-volume edition of his work appeared as *The New Testament in Modern English*. In 1963 his translation of Amos, Hosea, First Isaiah, and Micah appeared.

Notes

[1] Floyd V. Filson, "The Study of the New Testament," *Protestant Thought in the Twentieth Century*, ed. Arnold S. Nash (New York: The Macmillan Company, 1951), 51.

[2] Cited in F. F. Bruce, *The English Bible: A History of Translations* (New York: Oxford University Press, 1961), 136.

[3] "Reversers' Preface to The New Testament" in *The Holy Bible Containing the Old and New Testaments Translated out of the Original Tongues Being the Revised Version Set Forth AD 1881–1885 with Revised Marginal References* (New York: Oxford University Press, 1898), vii.

[4] Ibid.

[5] "Preface" to *The Holy Bible Containing the Old and New Testaments Translated out of the Original Tongues Being the Version Set Forth AD 1611 Compared with the Most Ancient Authorities and*

Revised AD 1881–1885, Newly Edited by the American Revision Committee AD 1901 (New York: Thomas Nelson & Sons, 1901), iii.

⁶ Ibid.

⁷ "The English of the Revised Standard Version of the New Testament," ibid., 53.

⁸ "The Revision of the English Bible," ibid., 13.

⁹ "Preface," *The Holy Bible: Revised Standard Version* (New York: Thomas Nelson & Sons, 1952), iv.

¹⁰ "Preface to the New English Bible," in *The New English Bible with the Apocrypha* (Oxford: Oxford University Press, 1970), v.

¹¹ "Introduction to the New Testament," ibid., vii.

¹² Ibid.

¹³ Helen Barrett Montgomery, "Translating the New Testament," *The Baptist* 6 (1925–1926): 51. Sharyn Dowd has recently discussed the work of Montgomery in an essay titled "Helen Barrett Montgomery's Centenary Translation of the New Testament: Characteristics and Influences," *Perspectives in Religious Studies* 19 (1992): 133-50.

¹⁴ "Introduction," *Centenary Translation of the New Testament* (Philadelphia: The American Baptist Publication Society, 1924), iii.

¹⁵ *New York Times*, 10 February 1924, sect. 1, pt. 2, p. 6. Cited in Roger A. Bullard, "Feminine and Feminist Touches in the Centenary New Testament," *The Bible Translator* 38 (1987): 119.

¹⁶ Bullard, 120-22.

¹⁷ She places quotation marks where translators usually place them in 1 Cor 1:12; 3:4; 6:12, 13; 8:1; 10:23; 2 Cor 10:10. She does not place quotation marks in 1 Cor 7:1. In addition, she has quotation marks in 1 Cor 8:5-11; 10:29-30; 14:34-35; 2 Cor 5:11-13; 10:1, 15; 11:1; Gal 1:10; 2:15; 5:11.)

¹⁸ See H. B. Montgomery, "Good Books for Busy Pastors," *The Baptist* 5 (1924–1925): 557-58.

¹⁹ Bruce, 214.

Chapter 13

Modern Translations Since the Revised Standard Version

Contemporary translations abound. The history of modern English translations may be compared with getting olives out of an old-fashioned, small-lipped olive jar. The first olive is difficult to dislodge, but the second and third are easier and succeeding olives come out with little difficulty. The translation of Goodspeed met with resistance, as did the Revised Standard Version. But from the time of publication of the Revised Standard Version in the middle of the twentieth century to the present, approximately thirty English translations of the entire Bible have appeared and nearly as many renderings of the New Testament alone. It would seem that out of these many translations one would have gotten it right! The history of Bible translations teaches us that it is not a matter of getting it right. In a symposium marking the 175th anniversary of the founding of the American Bible Society, Donald A. Carson compared Bible translations with educational choice where there are few absolute "rights" and "wrongs."

> Shall I send my children to the local school? to a private school? to a parochial school? to a junior college? to a state university? to a private university? Appropriate answers vary from child to child, from city to city, according to the resources available. Whatever decision parents choose, there are entailments with which they simply must live. So it is with translation. It is impossible to achieve perfection in all the possible *desiderata* simultaneously. So responsible translators learn as much as they can, make and correct their choices, and live with the entailments—recognizing that other translators, in different situations and with different skills, targeting

a quite different group of people, may make a different set of choices and be forced to live with a different set of entailments.[1]

Different Choices and Their Implications

The various translations imply different kinds of readers with different theological orientations and different levels of linguistic and literary competence. Different translations also imply different uses—ranging from private devotion and study to group worship. The question of anticipated readers and uses plays a part with other factors—the choice of the Hebrew and Greek texts to use in the translation and the degree of "consonance" between the original Hebrew and Greek and the English translation. Two specific questions today related to "consonance" are the treatment of the gender-bias inherent in the language of the Bible and the naming of the opponents of Jesus and the early church (referred to as "the Jews" in the King James Version) in the New Testament.

Most contemporary translations use Hebrew and Greek texts taken by scholars to represent as closely as possible the original biblical texts.[2] Two translations that seek to maintain the text used by the translators of the King James Version are the New King James Version (1979) and the 21st Century King James Version (1994).[3] The expectation was that these translations would be used by conservative Christian readers who did not want to give up reading the King James Version but who were no longer comfortable with the language of the seventeenth century. By the time these translations were published, however, new translations had appeared (like the olives out of the bottle) that used scholarly Hebrew and Greek texts and were acceptable to conservative American Christians. In fact, the success of one of these translations (The New International Version [1973]) seems to have inspired the publication of the New King James Version. It was too late, though—the King James Version in its new transformations would not capture the readership of the old King James Version.

Once the question of the proper Hebrew and Greek text to use in translation is settled, the question of "consonance" between the original Hebrew and Greek and English translation arises. Until the end of the Second World War, the King James Version reigned, with some few readers appealing to the Revised Version and the American Standard Version. These translations are literal, more or less word-for-word from the Hebrew and Greek. Moffatt, Goodspeed, and Phillips saw their work as idiomatic, phrase-for-phrase efforts to reproduce the meaning of the Hebrew and Greek. Montgomery's was a moderately free or "dynamic" translation. The efforts of these early dynamic translations were given theoretical foundations by the work of Eugene Nida, Robert Bratcher, and their associates in the American Bible Society. *Good News for Modern Man* (1976; NT, 1966) is the best-known translation using the principle of "dynamic equivalence" or "functional equivalence." This translation had its beginning in the late 1950s with a "common language" Spanish translation directed toward millions of Indians living in areas from northern Mexico to southern Chile. The translation used the common language of the vast majority of Spanish-speaking people. With the success of the Spanish version, Robert Bratcher, a former Southern Baptist missionary to Brazil, was asked to prepare a sample translation of Mark's Gospel and then to translate the entire New Testament. This translation, *Good News for Modern Man*, quickly sold some twelve million copies, and a team of translators undertook an Old Testament translation. The complete Bible was published in 1976 as *The Good News Bible: The Bible in Today's English Version.*[4]

The questions of gender-biased language in the Bible and anti-Jewish language in the New Testament are being addressed in contemporary translations. The treatment of these matters in translation makes clear the difference between functional equivalence and formal equivalence. Translators who follow the principle of formal equivalence require readers to go to the world of the text to understand the translation in terms of the ancient world. Translators who follow the principle of functional equivalence bring the biblical text to the reader in terms of the reader's world. To some extent the attention to gender-biased language in the Bible is an English language problem, but it is also a problem that arises because of the strong patriarchy that marked not only the ancient world but also the history of the translation and interpretation of the Bible in the Western world. Prefaces to the New Revised Standard Version, the Revised English Bible, and the New Jerusalem Bible contain statements noting the concern for gender-inclusive language:

> During the almost half a century since the publication of the RSV, many in the churches have become sensitive to the danger of linguistic sexism. . . . The mandates from the Division [of Education and Ministry of the National Council of Churches of Christ] specified that, in references to men and women, masculine oriented language should be eliminated as far as this can be done without altering passages that reflect the historical situation of ancient patriarchal culture (New Revised Standard Version).

> The use of male-oriented language, in passages of traditional versions of the Bible which evidently applied to both genders, has become a sensitive issue in recent years; the revisers have preferred more inclusive gender reference where that has been possible without compromising scholarly integrity or English style (Revised English Bible).

> Considerable efforts have . . . been made, though not at all costs, to soften or
> avoid the inbuilt preference of the English language, a preference now found so
> offensive by some people, for the masculine; the word of the Lord concerns
> women and men equally (New Jerusalem Bible).

The preface to the New Revised Standard Version acknowledges that passages
in the Bible reflect "the historical situation of ancient patriarchal culture." The
problem with the Bible translations, then, is not simply the bias of English for the
masculine gender—the rendering of gender-inclusive terms ("humankind," for
example) in a gender-exclusive fashion ("man," for example). The problem is the
strong patriarchy that marked the culture of the ancient world. Added to the
ancient culture is the patriarchal world in which translation and interpretation of
the Bible has taken place. Translations alone, therefore, will not correct the
modern-day mistreatment of women. The biblical text, correctly translated, still
reflects a culture with a unilateral submission of women and an extensive power
differential between men and women. Churches that cannot distinguish between
God's gracious revelation and the ancient culture accept the patriarchal system as a
revelation from God and will not allow women to function in any capacity that
places them in a position of power greater than that of a man. Along with proper
translations and the highlighting of women who play important roles in the Bible
must come the recognition of the historical and cultural limitations of the world of
the Bible.

Another area where it is important to take account of the historical situation is
the naming of those who oppose Jesus and/or followers of the way (Jews who
became Jesus' followers). In formal-equivalence translations, they are named "the
Jews." Knowledge of the historical situation and a desire to bring the biblical text to
the reader in terms of the reader's world is bringing about a change in translation.
James A. Sanders has stated the case pointedly and persuasively:

> Since it is clear that Jesus was a Jew, that all his early followers were Jewish by
> birth, or by conversion to a sect of Judaism, and that the Dead Sea Scrolls have
> shown that Christian Judaism was as much a Jewish community as any other
> within the Jewish pluralism of the time, then the polemic within the NT against
> "the Jews" needs to be addressed for what it really was, instead of allowing the NT
> language of Christian hurt and rejection at the end of the first century to continue
> to color what was going on in the first half thereof. If Bible translations like the
> NRSV can legitimately "correct" exclusion on one level, caused by the patriarchal
> cultural trappings in the text, they ought to be able to "correct" exclusion on the
> broader level, so that the text reflects what was essentially an intramural Jewish

situation of the early first-century period. The narratives provide clear mirrors for Christians today to see their own humanity reflected in those around Jesus, instead of identifying with Jesus and dehumanizing his fellow Jews.

The real issue is whether biblical scholarship is prepared to "go public" with the truth about the crucial gap between record and event in the case of these canonical narratives of Christian origins. If we think we have arrived at that point, then we should offer historically dynamic translations or we should print in banner headlines across the top of the usual formal equivalence translations of the gospels and Acts that they were written decades after the events recounted and in a quite different situation with regard to Christianity's Jewish origins. The present falsehood, with all the pain and damage it has for centuries caused both Christians and Jews, cannot in good conscience be permitted to continue.[5]

Major Contemporary Translations

The Jerusalem Bible. In 1966 English-speaking Roman Catholic readers were presented with a translation of the Bible approved by the Roman Catholic Church and based not on the Latin Vulgate but on the original languages. It was based on the original languages not directly, but through a French translation of the Bible called La Sainte Bible. The name "Jerusalem," in fact, derives from the fact that the translation of the French original was connected with a school in Jerusalem. The French translation was completed between 1948 and 1954 by the French Dominicans of L'Ecole Biblique de Jerusalem in Israel; and the English translation was correlated with a 1956 one-volume of abridgment of the original French work. For some books, the initial draft was made from the French with subsequent comparison with the original languages, and for other books initial drafts were made from the original languages and simultaneously compared with the French.

The Jerusalem Bible exists in different editions: (1) the 1966 Jerusalem Bible; (2) a 1968 Readers Edition of the Jerusalem Bible; (3) the 1986 New Jerusalem Bible; and (4) a 1989 Readers Edition of the New Jerusalem Bible. The Jerusalem Bible was developed primarily for study, with written introductions to biblical materials and explanatory notes. The 1968 Readers Edition was published in paperback with the extensive notes removed. It was designed for worship as well as study.

The 1966 Jerusalem Bible, in spite of its being a study Bible, followed the principle of functional equivalence. Doubtless this was due to its being based on the French translation and designed to possess style and literary flare. In fact it was in part criticism of the Jerusalem Bible as an interpretation rather than as a translation that led to the New Jerusalem Bible. The New Jerusalem Bible of 1986, therefore, was pointedly a translation from the ancient languages, using the French translation only when the words of the ancient manuscripts were not clear themselves. It is a formal-equivalence translation designed for study rather than for worship or private devotional use. The Readers Edition of the New Jerusalem Bible (1989) is clearly dependent on the format of the New Jerusalem Bible although it is designed for worship and for study.

The question of inclusive language had become important by the time the New Jerusalem Bible was produced, and a conscious attempt was made to be inclusive in its translation—although it followed the principle of formal-equivalence. A study of the way that the New Jerusalem Bible translates the Greek word *anthropos* is illuminating. One scholar has selected 100 instances where the word must be translated in a gender-inclusive way to be faithful to its use in the original. The Jerusalem Bible translates it in a gender-inclusive fashion ("human," "people," "person," "one," etc.) 48 percent of the time, while the New Jerusalem Bible translates it in an inclusive fashion 93 percent of the time.[6]

The Jerusalem Bible and the New Jerusalem Bible are alike in their lack of sensitivity to the problem of the naming of the opponents of Jesus and the early church in the New Testament. In the great majority of the 195 uses of *hoi Iudaioi* (literally "the Jews") both the Jerusalem Bible and the New Jerusalem Bible use "the Jews" and with consistency use the marker "Jewish" for all things Jewish ("the Jewish Passover" in John 2:13; "a Jewish festival" in John 5:1, and so on).

The New American Standard Version. The New American Standard Version (1971) and the New American Standard Version, Updated (1995) are attempts by the Lochman Foundation (dedicated to Christian education, evangelization, and Bible translation) to carry on the legacy of the American Standard Version. The foundation aims to provide translations that are accurate and faithful to the original languages in both meaning and word order, but the aim is also to provide more "modern" translations—*new* forms of the American Standard Versions.

The New American Standard Version is most radical in its attempt to provide a formal-equivalence translation of the ancient biblical text. This makes the translation particularly helpful for a person translating the Hebrew of the Old Testament and Greek of the New Testament. However, the slavish attention to the word order of the ancient texts makes the translation unacceptable for study by one who does not work with the Hebrew and Greek. Translation into the ancient word order risks confusion and distortion of the message. Moreover, the wooden and stilted style of the translation makes it unsuitable for public worship.

The New American Standard Version, Updated is a slight modification of the New American Standard Version. It removes obviously archaic language ("thee" and "thou") and makes some concession to English word order. It still desires to be as literal as possible, even if it is somewhat less wooden than the New American Standard Version. The questions of inclusive language and nuanced treatment of references to "the Jews" are not questions of interest to the New American Standard Version and the New American Standard Version, Updated.

The Living Bible and The New Living Translation. The popularity of the Living Bible (1971) and the New International Version (1973) shows that conservative evangelical Christians are not wed to rigid formal-equivalence translations. The Living Bible was produced by Kenneth Taylor, a seminary-trained publisher who was not satisfied with the American Standard Version and wanted to restate the biblical authors' thoughts in words used by contemporary readers. Two related matters are important for understanding and appreciating Taylor's work. First of all, the Living Bible is really a paraphrase. A paraphrase is more than a translation. A paraphrase does more than translate thought-for-thought. A paraphrase fills in the "gaps" in thought that readers normally fill in when they a read a text. The "gaps" may be filled in from different perspectives. The second important point, therefore, is that Taylor's perspective is that of "rigid evangelicalism." For Taylor and his readers, for example, salvation in terms of future rewards in heaven is a major focus. Romans 1:16 in the Living Bible, then, replaces "salvation" with "bringing all who believe to heaven." And in Galatians 5:11, Ephesians 3:21, and 1 Timothy 2:7 the phrase "plan of salvation" replaces phrases such as "the offense of the cross" and "the true faith."

The Living Bible is not concerned with the question of inclusive language. It uses "brothers" instead of "brothers and sisters" and "man" instead of "one" or "a human being." The naming of the enemies of Jesus and the early church, though, is more enlightened than contemporaneous translations. In place of the traditional "the Jews," the Living Bible has expressions such as "the Jewish leaders," "the people," or "the local Jewish leaders."

The New Living Translation is a translation in the tradition of the Living Bible, but it is a fresh translation by ninety evangelical scholars. It is in the tradition of the Living Bible in that it is free translation—not as free as the Living Bible, but consciously a functional-equivalence translation. The Hebrew and Greek texts used are the texts used by contemporary translators generally. (The Living Bible was a paraphrase from an English base.) The translation attempted to address deficiencies pointed out by critics of the Living Bible. It is less periphrastic and less theologically biased than the Living Bible. It continues an enlightened naming of the enemies of Jesus and the early church, with even fewer uses of "the Jews" than the Living Bible. One matter emphasized by the translators of the New Living

Translation but ignored by the Living Bible is the use of inclusive language. An attempt was made to fit the translation to a modern audience that tends to read male-oriented language as applying only to males. "Brothers" is translated as "brothers and sisters" where both men and women are intended. The pronoun "he" or "him" is replaced by plural pronouns or otherwise made inclusive when females and males are intended.

The New International Version. The New International Version (1973) is one of the most popular versions produced in the twentieth century. It is the result of the desire of evangelical scholars to produce a critically-accurate translation that would be acceptable to conservative Christians who would not use the Revised Standard Version. The decade-long project of translation began with studies by committees of the Christian Reformed Church and the National Association of Evangelicals. On the basis of these studies, a group of scholars met to plan for a new conservative translation. A fifteen-member committee on Bible translation was formed, the New York Bible Society (now the International Bible Society) offered to underwrite the project, and a careful plan was devised to insure that the translation would be conservative, scholarly, and readable. Translators were required to indicate adherence to a statement indicating a high view of biblical authority. The work of teams of translators was submitted to an editorial committee and then submitted to the committee on Bible translation for revision. This committee submitted the work to consultants for judgment on stylistic matters.

The New International Version is conservative not only in theological terms. It is conservative in terms of the text that is used in translation. Of course, there was no thought to use the text on which the King James Version was based. As scholars, the translators were aware of developments in textual criticism and consulted the critical texts used by other scholarly translators. But the New International Version claims to be based on an eclectic text. That is, scholars felt free to make their own decisions on specific textual questions. In terms of passages that had been the subject of debate because of the way they were translated by the Revised Standard Version, the New International Version is conservative (for example, in Isaiah 7, the New International Version presents the translation "virgin" rather than "young woman"—but in other places the word is translated as "young woman"). Still, the translation is also modern—without being offensive to those whose ears have trained by the rhythm and sounds of the King James Version.

The New International Readers Version (1996) is designed to make the Bible accessible to readers with limited literacy in English. This translation is based on the text of the New International Version. Sentences are shortened and simplified, and difficult and long words have been modified. The version is aimed at young

The very difficult issue of gender bias in language use was addressed in each version, but success varies from passage to passage within each work and between works, with the REB sometimes offering elegant, fresh readings where the NRSV stays with more traditional renderings, while in other passages the NRSV presents superior readings to those of the REB. Although results on this point are uneven in both new versions, either one presents a real advance over the earlier RSV and the NEB. Both show a fine "ear" for English, offering improved readability for public contexts, with the REB winning out over the NRSV primarily because of its reliance on dynamic equivalence that produces a more idiomatic English text. For the same reason, the NRSV will continue to be preferred by those who use the text with some concern for the original language structures in mind. The NRSV sounds more "familiar," a plus for some in liturgical situations, while the REB may be more enlightening.[8]

The New Testament and Psalms: An Inclusive Version. In 1995 a new version of the New Revised Standard Version of the New Testament and Psalms was published (*The New Testament and Psalms: An Inclusive Version*), one that intends to be radically inclusive. The text of the New Revised Standard Version was edited to

> replace or rephrase all gender-specific language not referring to particular historical individuals, all pejorative references to race, color, or religion, and all identifications of persons by their physical disability alone, by means of paraphrase, alternative renderings, and other acceptable means of conforming the language of the work to an inclusive idea.[9]

The New Revised Standard Version had used inclusive language where the original did not intend to exclude male or female ("brothers and sisters" for "brothers," "one" for "he," for example). The new version continues this practice but also uses gender-inclusive language for God. Further, it attempts to remove all negative references—race, color, religion, physical disability, and so on. For example, all references to darkness as a metaphor for evil are subtracted because they might be construed as racist. The editors indicate that they are attempting to anticipate developments that will take place in the use of the English language. Perhaps the substitution of "father-mother" for "father" will be the change most questioned by readers. In the introduction the editors defend this change:

> The church does not believe that God is literally a father, and understands "father" to be a metaphor, the metaphor "father" is rendered in this version by a new metaphor, "Father-Mother." This new metaphor is not even understandable as a literal statement and can be understood only in a metaphorical way. One cannot be literally a "Father-Mother," so the

metaphor allows the mind to oscillate between the picture of God as "Father" and the picture of God as "Mother," the mind attributing both fatherly and motherly attributes to God.

The Message. Eugene Peterson's *The Message* (1993), a paraphrase of the New Testament, has become a popular version of the Bible. It may be compared with J. B. Phillips's *The New Testament in Modern English*. In appearance, the two are alike. Phillips printed verse numbers only at the first line of each section (with the text appearing as a modern book) while Peterson omits verse numbers altogether. The language of both is fresh, commonly spoken English (of England in the case of Phillips, of America in the case of Peterson). The use of inclusive language in Peterson's work and the lack of inclusive language in the work of Phillips are due to the different epochs in which they appeared.

Both translations are interpretations, with Peterson's moving beyond an idiomatic translation into a paraphrase. As indicated earlier, a paraphrase is more than a thought-for-thought translation. It fills in "gaps" that readers ordinarily complete. Peterson will add short phrases to the text to help clear up confusion. In Matthew 1:18, for example, Peterson adds a parenthetical explanation for Joseph's confusion: "Before they came to the marriage bed, Joseph discovered she was pregnant. (It was by the Holy Spirit, but he didn't know that.)"

Peterson, as Phillips, was a pastor. He spent nearly three decades as a Presbyterian minister in Bel Air, Maryland. After retiring from the pastorate he became professor of spiritual theology at Regent College in Vancouver, BC. He has published a number of books on spirituality and this interest in spirituality is clearly involved at points in the translation.

Some renderings of Peterson have been spoken of as "simply strange."[10]

Romans 15:13—May the God of green hope fill you up with joy.
Romans 16:20—Enjoy the best of Jesus!
Galatians 6:13—All their talk about the law is gas.

Peterson's attempt to use lively metaphoric language will make the translation more dynamic for readers who must already know the street language employed by Peterson or who must search for the point of comparison (in the metaphor "the God of green hope," for example). The following translation from James (2:14-19) illustrates the work of Peterson.

Dear friends, do you think you'll get anywhere in this if you learn all the right words but never do anything? Does merely talking about faith indicate that a person really has it? For instance, you come upon an old friend dressed in rags and half-starved and say, "Good morning, friend! Be clothed in Christ! Be filled with the Holy Spirit!" and walk off without providing so much as a coat or a cup of soup—where does that get you? Isn't it obvious that God-talk without God-acts is outrageous nonsense?

I can already hear one of you agreeing by saying, "Sounds good. You take care of the faith department, I'll handle the works department."

Not so fast. You can no more show me your works apart from your faith than I can show you my faith apart from my works. Faith and works, works and faith, fit together hand in glove. Do I hear you professing to believe in the one and only God, but then observe you complacently sitting back as if you had done something wonderful? That's just great. Demons do that, but what good does it do them? Use your heads! Do you suppose for a minute that you can cut faith and works in two and not end up with a corpse on your hands?

Peterson handles the catalogue of sins in 1 Corinthians 6:9-10 and 1 Timothy 1:9-10 in an instructive way. In these passages the Greek word that can be translated "homosexual" is used. The King James Version uses the expressions "abusers of themselves with mankind" or "them that defile themselves with mankind." The New Revised Standard Version uses the term "sodomites." Apparently Peterson sees the catalogues of sins in the two passages as a way of speaking out against all sorts of abuses and he translates the passages in an inclusive fashion—omitting the specific references:

> Don't you realize that this is not the way to live? Unjust people who don't care about God will not be joining his kingdom. Those who use and abuse each other, use and abuse sex, use and abuse the earth and everything in it, won't qualify as citizens in God's kingdom. (1 Cor 6:9-10)

> It's obvious, isn't it, that the law code isn't primarily for people who live responsibly, but for the irresponsible, who defy all authority, riding roughshod over God, life, sex, truth, whatever! (1 Tim 1:9-10)

The Contemporary English Version. The Contemporary English Version (1995) began with Barclay Newman of the American Bible Society. Newman had assisted in the translation of the *Good News Bible* and in the mid-1980s he began to study popular forms of the English language to determine the sort of language people were then speaking and hearing. In 1986, a collection of illustrated Scripture passages for children was published and was warmly received. This encouraged the publication of a translation of the New Testament in 1991 (the 175th anniversary of the American Bible Society) and the entire Bible in 1995. The translators

wanted to produce a text faithful to the meaning of the original and used the scholarly editions of the Hebrew and Greek texts as the basis for their translation.
However, the translators were primarily concerned about the effect of public reading of the Bible. Three principles shaped the translation in this regard: (1) The
Bible should be easy for an inexperienced reader to read aloud. Attention was given
to line breaks to assist understanding and reading on the part of readers and hearers. (2) The translation should be understandable to those with little familiarity
with biblical language. (3) It should also be understood and enjoyed by English
speakers no matter what their religious or educational background. As indicated
earlier, the Contemporary English Version was very successful in its attempt at
gender-inclusive language; the translation was also successful in its attempt to rid
itself of complex theological language. Words such as "righteousness" and "redemption" are avoided in favor of simple phrases that express the same theological truths.
Figures of speech that might be unfamiliar to readers are put into familiar language.
Sometimes expressions are replaced by different figurative language. Stephen's
rebuke in Acts 7:51—"You stiff-necked people, with uncircumcised hearts and
ears!"—is rendered "you stubborn and hardheaded people!" Sometimes the figurative language is put into literal language. In 1 Thessalonians 4:14, "those who had
fallen asleep in him" is translated "his followers who have already died."

Conclusion

As this chapter shows, many people have invested their lives in the understanding
and translation of the Bible so it can be read in English. Today's scholars know
more about the original languages, are better prepared to reconstruct the original
text, and are more capable of putting the original languages into contemporary
English than ever before. Confidence in the work that biblical scholars have done is
more than justified. But the scholars themselves would be the first to caution that
no translation is perfect or can be treated as a final work. The English language will
change. More will become known about biblical Hebrew and Greek. Perhaps new
biblical manuscripts will be discovered—such as the Dead Sea Scrolls in 1947.

William Tyndale gave good up-to-date instruction in his prologue to the first
printed English New Testament. He said that if other men "perceive in any places
that I have not attained the very sense of the tongue, or meaning of the Scripture,
or have not given the right English word," they must "put to their hands to amend
it, remembering that so is their duty to do." He continues by declaring that "we
have not received the gifts of God for ourselves only, or for to hide them: but for to

bestow them unto the honoring of God and Christ, and edifying of the congregation, which is the body of Christ."[11]

Pastors and teachers are frequently asked, "What Bible should I choose?" Sometimes the Bible is for the person asking the question, sometimes for a friend as a gift. The answer is related to the factors listed at the beginning of this chapter: How will the Bible be used? Will the Bible be the only version used or will it be one among multiple versions? Where is the reader located in terms of reading ability, theological orientation, etc.?

When a reader is already familiar with the King James Version or another translation using the principle of formal equivalence, a translation following the principle of functional equivalence will be exciting and helpful. J. B. Phillips's *Letters to Young Churches* in an earlier day, *Good News For Modern Man* in the second half of the twentieth century, and *The Contemporary English Version* today are most appealing and helpful for those already familiar with a translation like the King James Version, the Revised Standard Version, or the New Revised Standard Version. On the other hand, readers may begin with popular functional-equivalence translations and move to more formal-equivalence translations. Regardless, formal-equivalence translations can be used profitably in conjunction with the functional-equivalence translations.

The question of what translation(s) to choose is related to its intended use. Is the Bible being read as part of an ongoing reading program? If so, the ease of reading, the flow of the narrative, the arrangement of poetic structure, and so on will be important. Is the Bible being read in preparation for teaching or preaching? Then attention will be limited to smaller passages and to the details within those passages. In this case, a number of different translations is advised. Is the Bible being read in public worship? If so, a translation that pays careful attention to the rhythm and style of the English language is important.

Translations offered today are successful in partially bringing the world of the text into the world of the reader. For these functional-equivalence translations, the readers' sensibilities, vocabulary, and worldview are primary. Translations that attempt to bring the reader into the world of the text are also offered. These formal-equivalence translations are important, because no translation can bring the ancient text completely into the world of contemporary readers. Readers must themselves move back and forth from the world of the text and their own world. In the process, different translations will be helpful, particularly if readers are aware of the differences between the translations and if they are willing to give the time and effort necessary for understanding and appreciating the message of the Bible.

Walter Harrelson, a well-respected Baptist student and teacher of the Hebrew Bible, has testified to the necessity of bringing the reader to the ancient text and bringing the text into the contemporary world:

> I am passionate about Bible translation because I have gained insight into virtually all aspects of what it means to be a responsible and free human being through the literature, imagery, and thought of the Bible. I have never been able to draw a firm line between "then" and "now," because the world I know today has so many similarities—in matters that count—with the biblical world. That frequently makes me an oddity in contemporary settings, but I can't help but draw much of my understanding of politics, ecology, social relations, and moral perceptions from the strange mix of biblical literature and thought.
>
> Since the above is true, I have always wanted to work at the question of how best to render the biblical texts into contemporary language and imagery. What is at stake is the very meaning of human life, of my life. . . .
>
> The translator should work to accomplish a plain task: to bring the reader to the text as the text is likely to have seized thoughtful hearers in its time(s), while at the same time bringing the text into the contemporary world with that world's different language, thought, imagery, prejudices, and the like. Translation is always working to enable the two worlds to overlap as much as possible. The slogan attributed to Jehuda ben Ilai still stands: "One who translates literally, lies; one who adds to the text, blasphemes." Translators carry out their perilous assignment between those two poles.[12]

Notes

[1] Donald A. Carson, "New Bible Translations: An Assessment and Prospect," *American Bible Society Symposium Papers on The Bible in the Twenty-first Century*, ed. Howard Clark Kee (Philadelphia: Trinity Press International, 1993), 66.

[2] The Hebrew text is a scholarly edition (printed in R. Kittel's *Biblia Hebraica*) based on the Codex Leningrad. However, scholars are also using biblical manuscripts (especially the Dead Sea Scrolls) and versions other than Hebrew in recovering the original text. The Greek text is a scholarly edition of the Greek New Testament (usually an edition of the United Bible Societies Greek New Testament that is essentially the same as the Nestle/Aland Greek New Testament—The Greek New Testament edited by Kurt Aland, Matthew Black, Carlo M. Martini, Bruce M. Metzger, and Allen Wikgren, in cooperation with the Institute for New Testament Textual Research, Münster/Westphalia). These scholarly editions provide a text that the editors believe is closest to the original, but they also contain critical apparatuses with alternate readings found in Greek manuscripts, versions, and the church fathers. The Greek text of the United Bible Societies and Nestle/Aland are not followed slavishly and differences may be observed between translations such as the New English Bible and the Revised Standard Version. Differences even exist between the New English Bible and the Revised English Bible and between the Revised Standard Version and the New

Revised Standard Version. Notes in these translations indicate variations in the texts used in translation.

³ The text used by the translators of the King James Version represented what was contained in the majority of the Greek manuscripts available. A text criticism based on this practice takes the position that the correct reading is the one contained in the majority of the manuscripts. The majority rules. The more acceptable theory of textual critics recognizes that we have copies of copies of Greek manuscripts, with each manuscript descending from an earlier manuscript. "Families" of manuscripts may be discerned with some families being older and more authentic than other families. Manuscripts representing these older and more authentic families carry more weight—even though they may be less numerous than manuscripts from other families.

⁴ Donald A. Carson indicates that the "widespread recognition of the primacy of dynamic equivalence (increasingly referred to as 'functional equivalence') as the best controlling model in Bible translation" is a "remarkable reversal." He indicates that until the end of World War II, readers who did not use the King James Version used the Revised Version, the American Standard Version, or perhaps the Douay Version. These are literal translations. When the Good News Bible first appeared, most conservative readers roundly condemned it. Just a few years later, however, these same readers expressed themselves as satisfied with the New International Version, whose philosophy of translation is hard to differentiate from that of the Good News Bible. Carson concludes that "dynamic (or functional) equivalence has triumphed, whether the expression itself be embraced or not; even among translators who think of their work as more 'literal,' its influence is pervasive." Carson himself judges that "by and large, this has been a good thing" ("New Bible Translations: An Assessment and Prospect," 40-41). In the catalogue of recent translations given below, the place of the translation on the spectrum between "literal translation" and "free translation" will be indicated.

⁵ James A. Sanders, "The Hermeneutics of Translation," *Explorations* 12/2 (1998): 1. David G. Burke, a representative of the American Bible Society, has examined the way that the expression "the Jews" [*hoi Ioudaioi*] is handled in English translations. The expression is used 195 times in the New Testament. Those translations following the principle of formal equivalence tend to translate the expression literally "the Jews." The Revised Standard Version, according to Burke, "tends consistently to use 'the Jews' and the formula, 'x of the Jews,' in very wooden ways, and demonstrates a lack of sensitivity to this issue." He indicates that this matter was evidently not of major importance (as was inclusive language) to the translators of the New Revised Standard Version. Translators who use the principle of dynamic equivalence are particularly concerned to bring the Bible into the world of the reader, and since "the Jews" support an anti-Jewish hatred today, translators seek another way to speak of opponents of Jesus and/or Jesus' followers. Burke suggests that the first functional equivalence English translation of the American Bible Society (The Good News Bible) "was clearly ahead of its time in pioneering translational breakthroughs in the area of providing more nuanced sensitivity in the handling of these [195] passages." The first edition of the Good News Bible (1976) has "the Jews" in only one-fourth of the cases where *hoi Ioudaioi* is used in the Greek, and the second edition (1992) makes further adaptation. It is the 1995 publication of the American Bible Society titled The Contemporary English Version that is singled out for special treatment by Burke: ". . . the CEV is further ahead of the other versions in the way in which it has been able to handle this issue with nuanced and sensitive language use." In only 9 of the 195 uses of *hoi Ioudaioi* (apart from the use in the title, "King of the Jews") does the CEV have "the Jews" (David G. Burke, "Translating *Hoi Ioudaioi* In The New Testament, " *Explorations* 9/2 (1995): 1-7).

[6] Herbert G. Grether, "Translators and the Gender Gap," *Theology Today* 47 (1990–1991): 301.

[7] Paige Patterson, "A 'Gender Neutral' NIV," *National Liberty Journal* 26 (May 1997), 22.

[8] Carole R. Fontaine, "The *NRSV* and the *REB*: A Feminist Critique," *Theology Today* 47 (1990–1991): 280.

[9] Victor Gold, Thomas Hoyt Jr., Sharon Ringe, et al., *The New Testament and Psalms: A New Inclusive Version* (Oxford University Press, 1995), viii-iv.

[10] Steven M. Sheeley and Robert N. Nash Jr., *The Bible In English Translation: An Essential Guide* (Nashville: Abingdon Press, 1997), 91.

[11] Cited in F. F. Bruce, *The English Bible: A History of Translations* (New York: Oxford University Press, 1961), 32.

[12] Walter Harrelson, "What Translation Is," *Religious Studies News: Society of Biblical Literature Edition* 3 (July 2002): 5-6.

Chapter 14

Varieties of Readings: Credulous, Critical, and Creative Approaches

Reading of a biblical text begins with readers making sense of the words of a text in terms of the readers' acquaintance with the words and the readers' ability to process the words and sentences of the text. Other questions are also at work allowing readers to discover and create meaning. What sort of text is being read? What is the text about? What is the Bible? How does the Bible mean? Different kinds of readings are possible.

Contemporary reading and appreciation of the Bible benefit from knowledge of the different kinds of readings that have been used in the history of interpretation. Three basic models exist: a credulous reading that sees the text as an oracle, as the word of God in a very real if not literal sense; a critical reading that sees the text as an object, a human product requiring such things as knowledge of the original socio-historical setting of the text to understand it; and a creative reading that sees the Bible as literary art allowing readers to find and discover meaning and significance that match their need and competence.

In this chapter, we will begin with the reading of the Bible that developed as the canons of the Hebrew Bible and the New Testament developed—the Bible as word of God, as divine revelation, or as oracle. In the epoch when this model of reading reigned, historical and literary aspects of biblical texts were obvious, and these aspects in their turn (and after a long period of time) moved from the periphery to the center of interest. But historical-critical and literary-critical modes of reading developed against the horizon of the dogmatic approach, and hermeneutical strategies were developed to allow the Bible to continue to speak as personal address. At the present time, combinations of transformations of the oracular model and historical-critical and literary-critical models are being found useful in approaches to reading found in movements such as liberation and feminist theology. The Bible is seen as addressing the present needs and situation of the reader. The readers' own perspective and social location are important ingredients in the reading.

Credulous Readings: The Bible as Oracle

The Bible as a canon of Scripture came into existence because believers heard the voice of God speaking to them in certain writings. Thus, the formation of the Bible as canon (the Hebrew Bible and the Christian Bible) and the assumptions as to what Scripture was and meant and how it was to be read were interdependent. As the Bible was created by stitching together songs, prayers, sermons, narratives, and other sorts of writing, it became something more than a collection of ancient documents. It became one book and readers read that book in a special way. Four of these special ways of reading may be defined:

(1) The Bible was read as one great book of instruction, with everything in the Bible having immediate relevance for readers. Even the historical narratives were directly applicable. The narratives recounted things that actually happened, but they were written not for historical purposes but for purposes of instruction. Reading, then, is designed to discern vital lessons for the readers' own lives. Paul's treatment of the Israelites' wandering in the desert illustrates the attitude. In his letter to the Corinthians, Paul indicated that what happened to the Israelites in the wilderness "happened to them to serve as an example, and they were written down to instruct us upon whom the end of the ages have come" (1 Cor 10:11).

(2) The Bible was read with the assumption that there was no mistake in the Bible—and that the Bible was perfectly harmonious. Readers, then, begin with the conviction that apparent disagreements are illusions to be clarified by proper interpretation. More importantly, readers find meaning in every detail. Nothing is said in vain or for rhetorical flourish. Apparently insignificant details—repetition and unusual words or grammatical forms, for example—are fraught with meaning. The statement in Genesis 25:27 that Jacob dwelt "in tents" supports the notion that Jacob—unlike his brother Esau—had some sort of schooling. The plural "tents" implies at least two tents, one for home and one for a school! The perfection of Scripture extended to the conduct of biblical

heroes and the content of biblical teaching. Rachel must not have really stolen her father's household gods as Genesis 31:19 indicates. She must have taken them for some worthy purpose such as to protect her father from sin.

(3) The Bible was read as a writing with cryptic or hidden meaning; it means more than it says. According to Philo, for example, where the Bible speaks of Abraham, it refers to more than a historical figure. Abraham is a symbol for the virtue-loving soul. For early Christian readers, Cain's brother Abel was a foreshadowing of Christ.

(4) The Bible is divinely inspired. This assumption is related to assertions in Scripture that particular portions of Scripture come from God. "Thus says the Lord," for example, is used by many prophets to introduce their proclamation. As the Hebrew Bible came to be canonized, the idea of divine provenance was extended to the entirety of Scripture.[1]

Early Christian leaders gave conscious attention to the question of appropriate ways of reading the Bible. Ireneaus of Lyon (c. 130–200), for example, gave attention to methods of Bible reading and the critera to be used to guide and validate proper reading. He acknowledged historical, typological, and allegorical readings, and he propounded the "rule of faith" as a guide and validation of reading, especially in light of the Gnostic heretical denial or devaluation of the Hebrew Scriptures and the creator God of those Scriptures. The couplet that was devised in the West distinguishes four different ways of reading:

> *Littera gesta docet, quid credas allegoria,*
> *moralis quid agas, quo tendas anagogia*

> ("The letter teaches the events, allegory what you are to believe, the moral sense what you are to do, anagoge whither you are to strive.")

John Cassian (died c. 435) provided illustration of these four sorts of reading with the use of the word "Jerusalem." When Jerusalem is mentioned in the Bible, it means a Jewish city in the literal or historical sense, the Church of Christ in the allegorical sense, the human soul in the tropological (moral or anthropological sense) and the heavenly city in the anagogical (eschatological) sense.[2]

Private devotional readings and liturgical and homiletical settings, functions, and readings of the Bible are related to the Bible seen as oracle. In devotional reading, readers read Scripture expecting to receive a directly relevant word from God.

The relationship between the text and the reader is immediate. The reader does not distance the text historically in order to understand the original content and message. Rather God speaks to the reader directly through the words of Scripture. Lectionaries were developed when the Bible was seen as a coherent book of divine instruction, and selections were made from the Old Testament and New Testament in light of perceived prophecy-fulfillment relationships. Sermons related to these texts are designed not to uncover historical meaning but to reveal the word of God. Hence, a homiletical reading seeks for the theme in God's plan that ties the texts together.

The Bible itself suggests that things written in the Bible may be seen to have deeper meanings when they are read in the light of future things in God's work of salvation. In the New Testament, Adam is see as a type of Christ (Rom 5:14) and the exodus is a type of baptism (1 Cor 10:2). Roman Catholic scholars use the term *sensus plenior* (fuller sense) to speak of "the deeper meaning intended by God but not clearly intended by the human author, that is seen to exist in the words of Scripture when they are studied in the light of further revelation or of development in the understanding of revelation."[3]

Critical Readings: The Bible as Historical Product

With the historical-critical paradigm, aspects of the biblical text that were dormant in the oracular paradigm became central. Authors and original readers, the circumstances of writing, the purposes of the writing, and other historical factors are seen as important. The historical explanation of cause supplements or replaces the theological explanation. A historical-critical reading of a text, then, treats the text as a product with historical causes rather than an oracle with direct divine cause. When the reader reads the Bible with historical sensitivity, different moments in the historical flux may be emphasized. Source criticism reads biblical texts as the result of earlier oral and written sources and/or as the source for later texts. Students who are sensitized to the methods of source analysis, for example, will see the recurrence of the names of God in the narratives of the Hebrew Bible ("Yahweh," "Elohim," "Shaddai," "El Shaddai," "El Elyon," etc.) as reflecting different sources. Doublets and repetitions and stylistic differences that are seen in the oracular paradigm as conveying special insight and information are accounted for in source criticism by the existence and use of different sources.

Tradition-historical criticism encourages readers to classify traditions according to formal linguistic and literary features, to correlate the traditions with specific settings within the life of the community, and to note stages in the development of the tradition. Stories of the great heroes of Israel (the stories of Abraham in Genesis 12–25 and the stories of David's rise to power in 1 Samuel 16–2 Samuel 5, for example) are read in light of their origins as shorter, independent accounts and their development into cycles or collections centering on a specific period or character. The various traditions are read in light of the meaning and significance of each individual unit at its successive stages.

To read in the light of form criticism is to identify the literary genre or form of the unit being read or studied and to follow the conventions of that form in reading. The form is identified in light of concrete historical and sociological contexts. The individual units of the tradition are removed from the literary context in which they are found and set in the literary, historical, and sociological context of their formation. The history of particular forms and traditions may the focus of reading. Controversy stories in the Gospels, for example, may be read in light of controversies in the church at the time of the formation of the stories.

Reading sensitized by redaction criticism looks at units and entire books of the Bible from the perspective of the process of editing (redaction). How do changes in the accounts of the story of Israel and the story of Jesus Christ reflect the context of the editors of the material? The work of a redactor is evident in the book of Judges as the stories about various tribal heroes are arranged so that each illustrates the same pattern: the people sin, they are subjugated by their enemies, they cry to God and are saved by a "judge," they enjoy a period of rest, and the cycle begins again with the sin of the people. The fact that the theological perspective reflected in the book of Judges may be seen in all of the material from Joshua to 2 Kings suggests that the same redactor may have worked on this material.

A canonical reading is sensitive to the function or authority of the ancient tradition in the context in which it is cited. It is interested in the way that early authoritative traditions were adapted in new situations by the believing communities. Canonical readings recognize that the *Sitz-im-Leben* (life setting) of the Bible is the believing community and that the modern *Sitze-im-Leben* (life settings) of the Bible are the believing communities that are heirs to the original shapers of the literature.

Canonical readings also give attention to the canonical shaping. In the New Testament the separation of Acts from Luke by the Gospel of John results in the canonical reading of Luke as a Gospel alongside Matthew, Mark, and John. Canonically interpreted, the four Gospels are read as witnesses to the good news of Jesus Christ. Moreover, the placing of the Pauline epistles after the Gospels (although written before the Gospels) has these epistles serve as a commentary on the message found in the four Gospels.

A sociological reading of the Bible sees the Bible as a social document that reflects the changing social structures, functions, and roles in Israel and the early church. Reading the prophets in light of sociological insights will see the prophets as intimately involved in societal life with such involvement taking the form of either social maintenance or social change. Insiders sought to legitimize the establishment while outsiders challenged the establishment, condemning existing social conditions and demanding radical change. Apocalypticism and apocalyptic writings (the book of Revelation, for example) are illuminated when the seedbed of apocalypticism is seen as lying in an experience of social alienation and the feeling of deprivation.

Historical readings of the Bible are not necessarily opposed to a theistic worldview. Historical criticism can enable the believing critic to note the witness of the divine spirit in the historical witness of the Scriptures or to see historical method as the method allowing theology to share in and give shape to universal historical progress. Such a vision became difficult to maintain, however, with two bitter world wars and continuing social upheaval. Rudolf Bultmann's existential interpretation may be seen as an early response to the dilemma for interpretation posed by the crisis of historical criticism. The question of the meaning of all history was replaced with the question of the individual's encounter with historic events, and the theology of the Bible was limited to speaking in terms of human existence. Bultmann's approach was to look behind the biblical text to determine its existential content—either as a kerygmatic word (proclamation) of personal address or as a theological statement expressing publicly the consequence of the response to the kerygmatic word.

When biblical texts are read from the perspective of existential theology, they are read as speaking of God by speaking of human existence and as speaking of Christ by speaking of the salvation that Christ brings. The eschatology of the New Testament may be read kerygmatically (or existentially), in terms of actual individual existence. According to apocalyptic eschatology, the present age would be brought to an end shortly through a supernatural intervention. A final judgment would take place and people would be assigned to destinies either of bliss or torment. The early Christian expectation of an imminent eschaton turned out to be mistaken. Nevertheless, the ideas of apocalyptic eschatology can be interpreted in relation to the here and now of our own existence. Every individual stands before an imminent end—his or her own death. In their everyday decisions, individuals work out their own judgment as they lay hold on authentic being or lose authentic being.

Creative Readings: The Bible as Literary Art

The literary nature of the Bible has been noted by readers in epochs dominated by dogmatic and historical readings. Augustine, for example, was exponent of a dogmatic approach that saw soundness of doctrine and purity of life as the bases for reading and interpretation. These schemata required that much of the Bible be interpreted in a literary or symbolic fashion. "Whatever there is in the word of God that cannot, when taken literally, be referred either to purity of life or soundness of doctrine, you may set down as figurative."[4] In *On Christian Doctrine*, Augustine cites Song of Solomon 4:2: "Your teeth are like a flock of shorn ewes that have come up from the washing, whereof every one bears twins, and none is barren among them" as praise of the Church under the figure of a beautiful woman. He acknowledges that the reader learns no more from the figure than from plain language. "And yet," says Augustine, "I feel greater pleasure in contemplating holy men, when I view them as the teeth of the Church, tearing men away from their errors, and bringing them into the Church's body, with all their harshness softened down just as if they had been torn off and masticated by the teeth." Augustine questions why he views them with greater delight in a literary language. He does not answer the question, but he acknowledges that "it is pleasanter in such cases to have knowledge communicated through figures."[5]

Other chapters in this volume delineate different sorts of poetry in the Bible, treat major literary forms (historical narrative, prophecy, apocalyptic writing, wisdom literature, and letters) and define and illustrate figures of speech (simile, metaphor, metonymy, synecdoche, personification, hyperbole, understatement, irony, parable). This section will introduce readers to contemporary and more wide-ranging insights into structural readings, narrative readings, rhetoric, and the role of the reader in the process of reading.

Literary approaches to biblical texts in general began following the popularity of structuralist and formalist approaches to literature—including American New Criticism. These approaches protested the reduction of literary criticism to literary history. The understanding with which literary criticism should be concerned, according to New Criticism, is not equivalent to knowing why an author said what he said in a genetic or historical sense. Rather, it is equivalent to knowing what the author is saying and reasons for saying it in the sense of its artistic rational. When applied to the Bible, historical cause (as earlier theological cause) was replaced by literary cause or literary *relationship*. A structuralist reading of a biblical text gives attention to the deeper underlying patterns that account for the surface level of the text and to meanings that may be found in these deeper relationships.

The identification of character types and plot patterns in a story may assist in moving to a deeper level and to greater appreciation for what is going on in a story. The character types in a story are responsible for carrying the story along. The story of Jacob and the angel in Genesis 32:22-32 may be read in light of categories developed in the study of folklore. Participants in the story are defined in terms of the following character types: God is the "originator," Jacob is the "hero," and the angel is Jacob's "opponent." In the classical folktales, these character types interact in various ways: the "originator" may step in to help the "hero"; one or more "helpers" may be introduced into the plot; or the "hero" may succeed in the quest by his or her own efforts, and at the end be rewarded by the "originator." A literary critic has discovered that in the story in Genesis the normal patterns are not followed. The "originator" *and* "opponent" turn out to be God. The very God who sent Jacob on his journey is the God with whom Jacob wrestled all night and who finally blessed Jacob for his persistence in resisting God. In the case of the story of Jacob and the angel, the subversion of the normal rules of folktale produce a shocking and disturbing outcome that is theologically significant. Attention to the deeper level of relationships here is consistent with a central theme of much Old Testament narrative that avoids dualistic explanations of history and attributes both good and bad experiences to the providential guidance of God.[6]

A narrative reading gives attention to the narrative text in its final or canonical form in terms of its own story world. It does not attempt to reconstruct the sources behind the text, the original setting and audience, or the author's intention. Narrative reading is close reading that identifies conventional formal features of the text, such as plot, setting, characterization, point of view, and creative use of language. Narrative reading is not primarily interested in the deeper abstract level but in the surface level. It seeks to relate the formal features of the text to some overarching theme. Reading narrative as narrative, a reader will discover plot. Plot is the arrangement of events into a beginning, a middle, and an end, which together form a completed whole. The events in the plot move toward the resolution of some conflict. Ingredients of stories are characters, settings, and the strategies for moving the story along in an interesting way and involving the reader in the story. The story told by the narrator of Mark, according to the analysis of one group of scholars, is "a story full of gaps, rife with all forms of suspense, punctuated with puzzles and riddles to decipher—with characters who are amazed at developing events, with twists and turns, with paradoxes, and with great irony." But "a pattern of purpose" is to be seen in Mark—a pattern of purpose to be seen with the eyes of faith.

As when one looks at a puzzle, one may gaze at Mark for a long time in order finally to discern the fabric of God's rule in the way and in the places and in the people where Mark claims it to be present. In a sense, then, the narrator tells a story designed to lead the reader to experience all the joys and triumphs of the rule of God hidden in the present age amid the suffering and ambiguity of life—while awaiting Jesus' return in power and glory.[7]

To read the Bible as rhetoric is to read it in light of its nature as a means of persuasion. To read a biblical text from a rhetorical perspective involves determining the sort of persuasion involved (persuasion of the audience to make a judgment about events occurring in the past, to take some action in the future, or to honor or denigrate some person or quality) and noting how the literary devices and the total structure carry out a rhetorical function.

The prophets employed rhetoric effectively, and Paul's letter to the Galatians may be read as an "apologetic letter" that incorporates rhetorical devices familiar to the law court. Paul is the defendant, the Galatians play the role of the jury, and Paul's opponents are the accusers. The structure of the letter, then, is seen as incorporating the standard parts of a legal argument: introduction, statement of facts, main points to be made, proof, and conclusion.[8]

Attention to the rhetorical nature of biblical texts makes clear the importance of the audience to the writer. An audience or reader is envisioned by the writer in the composition of material designed to persuade. However, with all literature, readers are implied. In a reading that seeks the "implied reader" (the reader consciously or unconsciously intended by the author—to be reconstructed by the text), the textual data is primary. A question that might guide this sort of reading is the question as to how the reader implied by the text experiences the text as it unfolds. What does this reader know at the end that he or she did not know at the beginning, and how does previous knowledge influence the reading of later episodes? The reading of the conclusion of the Gospel of Mark may thus be illuminated by asking what the implied readers bring to the episode about the women fleeing the tomb and not telling anyone (Mark 16:8). Modern-day readers may come to different conclusions, with all of the conclusions based on the text. When readers focus on the negative examples of the disciples' behavior from earlier episodes, the conclusion emphasizes Jesus' abandonment by all his followers. When readers focus on the second part of the message of the young man ("But go, tell his disciples and Peter that he is going ahead of you to Galilee; there you will see him, just as he told you"), they are directed to the statement of Jesus in 14:28 about Jesus' going before the disciples to Galilee after his resurrection, and they know that they will be reconstituted as a community. With the prophecies of Mark 13 in mind (concerning the future of believers and the notation that the sons of Zebedee will share Jesus'

suffering), readers of the Gospel around the year AD 70 will realize that the followers of Jesus did indeed take up the cross.

The focus on the real reader in the contemporary process of reading enables us
to see the cooperation of the text and the actual reader in the actualization of the
text. Readers assume that a text makes sense as a linguistic and literary unit and
intuitively use their linguistic and literary competence in the process of actualization. When ambiguity arises, a reader becomes conscious of the process that is
being followed. When we read in 2 Samuel 13 that David's son Absalom has his
brother Ammon killed, we are able to make sense of the text. We know the appropriate categories and are able to work out the logic of cause and effect, since we
know from earlier information that Absalom is avenging Ammon's rape of Tamar,
their sister. But when we read, "David mourned for his son day after day" (2 Sam
13:37), we have a problem. Is it for the murdered Ammon that David mourns or
for the murderer, Absalom, who has been forced to flee to Geshur? What sense is a
reader to make? In the processing of the text, then, the reader will discover that the
text does not (indeed, cannot) make explicit all that must be known to make sense
of the text. Grammatical and syntactical structures and semantic information must
be identified and supplied by the actual reader. Coherence is the key to the deter-
mination of indeterminate grammatical and syntactical structures, the solution to
problems of ambiguity, and the establishment of motivation and order in the text.

When modern readers appreciate their own role in discovering and creating
meaning, they may seek to find meanings that complement and/or challenge conventional readings. In an early sermon as new minister of the First Baptist Church
of Greenville, South Carolina, Jeffrey Rogers read from the lectionary text of
2 Kings 5, "Now the Arameans on one of their raids had taken a young girl captive
from the land of Israel, and she served Naaman's wife. She said to her mistress, 'If
only my lord were with the prophet who is in Samaria! He would cure him of his
leprosy'" (vv. 2-3). Then Rogers suggested that when Jesus spoke of a little child in
Mark 10:15 ("Truly I tell you, whoever does not receive the kingdom of God as a
little child will never enter it") he was speaking of a little child like this girl who
served Naaman's wife. He was not speaking of a little girl made "of sugar and spice
and everything nice" but of a little girl "of a very different mettle . . . made of nails
and gold and everything bold."

Rogers reminded his hearers that after Jesus' inaugural sermon in the synagogue in Nazareth, our Lord said to those who praised his preaching, "There were
many people suffering from a dreaded skin disease who lived in Israel during the
time of the prophet Elisha; yet none of them was healed, but only Naaman the
Syrian" (Luke 4:27). When the good religious people of Nazareth heard these
words they became so angry that they turned against him on the spot and wanted

to kill him. This story about God's grace and healing power being accessible even to those who were Israel's historic enemies was more than Jesus' audience could take. And so they turned on him on the spot. Rogers said in his statement about a little child in Mark 10,

> Jesus doesn't mention this little girl made of nails and gold and everything bold, but that doesn't stop me from making the entirely outlandish suggestion that he was thinking of her—or someone very much like her—when he said, "I assure you that whoever does not receive the Kingdom of God like a child will never enter it." We have been taught over the centuries that when Jesus commended the faith of children he was talking about something like "trustful simplicity" or perhaps "teachable humility." But if you think about the young people whom we meet in the Bible, we sometimes see something quite different. It was David, the youngest of Jesse's sons and "just a boy," who stepped forward to say of the warrior Goliath, "I will go and fight him" (1 Sam 17:32), and he would not be dissuaded by the arguments of his brothers or King Saul. It was Mary, in her teens and unwed, who responded just as courageously, "Here am I, the servant of the Lord; let it be with me according to your word" (Luke 1:38). And it was her son who at age twelve amazed the teachers in the temple with "his understanding and his answers" to their questions (Luke 2:47). When we look at children portrayed in scripture we see much more than "trustful simplicity" or "teachable humility." We see more often qualities that amaze and confound the adults around them and sometimes even put them to shame. So we should not be surprised that in this morning's scripture passage we meet a little girl made of nails and gold and everything bold.[9]

An Old Testament scholar has pointed out that some aspects of Psalm 24 are at odds with the main point that the psalm affirms. (1) The psalm wants to affirm that the world as a whole is the LORD's possession. Verse one affirms that "the earth is the LORD's and all that is in it, the world, and those who live in it." But verse 3 challenges this view in speaking of the hill that belongs to God and of God's holy place. If all the world belongs to the LORD, in what sense can one hill belong to the LORD? If the whole world is holy by virtue of the LORD's possession, in what sense can one place be holy? (2) The affirmation in verse one that all who live on the earth belong to the LORD is challenged by the reference to warfare. That is, if the LORD must engage in battle against enemies, how can these enemies be said to be the LORD's? (3) The accession of the hill of the LORD proves that one is innocence (verse four); yet those who ascend the hill are in need of vindication (verse five). The psalm, however, does not show in what way those who ascend the hill of the LORD need vindication. (4) Those who worship on the hill are to have "clean hands and pure hearts" and not to lift up their souls to what is false. Yet the deity is not held to this standard. The deity is one who is mighty in battle. The qualities demanded of those worshiping, then, are not the same as the quality of the deity they worship—qualities that are praised.[10]

Feminist and Liberation Readings

Readers who seek to find in the Bible a liberating word for women have developed a variety of reading strategies to accomplish this agenda. Common to these strategies and readings is the observation that not only has a patriarchal bias influenced the history of biblical studies but that an androcentric and patriarchal bias is to be found in the biblical text itself. When contemporary readers attempt to make the patriachally-biased reading the proper reading (and call for women to submit graciously to men, for example), they are shaken by texts that declare the equality of men and women. How may contemporary readers be faithful to the biblical text and live without compromise in the twenty-first-century world?

The fact that biblical texts reflect a patriarchal bias can be dealt with by distinguishing between the contingent patriarchal dimensions of biblical texts and the enduring theological values expressed in those texts. Genesis 2–3 is an important text that reflects the view that women are inferior to men.[11] The male is created first and the female is created as a helper. The woman is the first to succumb to temptation. The divine judgment concerning the woman states: "I will greatly increase your pangs in child bearing; in pain you shall bring forth children, yet your desire shall be for your husband, and he shall rule over you" (Gen 3:16). Instead of giving attention to the historically-constrained aspects in a reading, the major religious and theological aspects may be emphasized. Genesis 2–3, then, may be read as teaching that alienation and estrangement are the result of sin. The good gift of sexuality—intended for fulfillment and self-transcendence—may become the means of oppression and deprivation.[12]

Another valuable procedure is to get behind the history of interpretation and to read the actual text afresh, seeking to bypass any patriarchal influences. It is possible, for example, to read Genesis 2–3 not as a justification of woman's inferiority but as an affirmation of a remarkable equality between the sexes. The arguments used for such a reading involve careful attention to the text: God created the first human without gender. It is only after the fall that hierarchy becomes a part of human existence as a consequence of disobedience. It is only after the woman is differentiated that the original human being acquires a gender. The word "helper" used to describe the woman is a term used often in reference to God and denotes not an inferior being but rather a superior being. The woman is decisive and assertive, but the man is passive and compliant.[13]

Another way to deal with texts that show women as subordinate to and derivative of men in the order of creation is to read those texts in light of countertexts that challenge the non-liberating texts. The account of creation in Genesis 2–3, for example, can be countered with the first account of woman's creation (Gen 1:26-27), in which the human being is described as both "male and female" and created in the image of God. Texts in the Bible show women who maintained positions of leadership and authority—Miriam, a prophet; Deborah, a prophet and judge; Huldah, a prophet who authorized a newly discovered text and Scripture; Phoebe, a deacon of the church of Cenchreae; Priscilla (Prisca), a coworker of Paul. One feminist Old Testament scholar has focused attention on the way that the speech and action of the midwives, Pharaoh's daughter, and Moses' mother shape the contours of the story of Pharaoh's attempts to mold history in Exodus 1:8–2:10. Women repeatedly foil and frustrate the strategies of Pharaoh.[14] A New Testament scholar has suggested that the androcentric perspective of the Gospel of Matthew may be altered by seeing the Gospel of Matthew through the stories of the woman with the hemorrhage (Matt 9:20-22) and especially the Canaanite woman (Matt 15:21-28). In Matthew, for the most part, "women are portrayed favorably. The important role of women and of Jesus' response to women supplicants strain the boundaries of the Gospel's patriarchal worldview."[15]

Pauline texts that seemed to denigrate females are countered by texts such as 1 Corinthians 11:11-12 (". . . in the Lord woman is not independent of man or man independent of woman. For just as woman came from man, so man comes through woman; but all things come from God") and Galatians 3:28 ("There is no longer Jew or Greek, there is no longer slave or free, there is no longer male and female for all of you are one in Christ Jesus").

The overwhelming and centuries-long influence of male-dominated political, social, academic, theological, and religious structures has made it necessary to detect androcentric tendencies in biblical translations, models of explanation, and interpretation so as to neutralize them. Critical attention must also be given to biblical texts themselves as they have supported these androcentric tendencies and traditions. A feminist reading will be suspicious. A simplistic credulous reading is not appropriate. Modern followers of Christ are no more supposed to believe that women are inferior to men than to believe that the earth is flat! The strategies suggested will inoculate readers against an uncritical acceptance of the patriarchal bias.

Liberation theology is a phenomenon that began in third world countries and it is marked by a way of reading the Bible that is akin to the reading of the Bible as oracle. Particular biblical texts that stress liberation are matched up with readers so as to give authoritative answers to critical questions faced by the poor and oppressed. The original meaning and the original context are left behind, and a new meaning is created in a new context by rereading. This process of recontextualization is a process found in the Bible itself. In the Gospel of Luke, there is an account of Jesus reading the Scripture in the synagogue at Nazareth and concluding with the statement: "Today this scripture has been fulfilled in your hearing" (Luke 4:21). In his letter to the churches of Galatia, Paul states that the situation of Abraham, who had two wives and two sons, one born to a slave woman and one to a free woman, is an allegory. Paul reads traditions from Genesis 16 and 21 in light of the new situation faced by the early church (Gal 4:21-31). In Isaiah 43:16-19, the prophet of the exile cites the experiences of the exodus and then declares, "Behold, I am doing a new thing; now it springs forth, do you not perceive it? I will make a way in the wilderness and rivers in the desert." The past informs the exiles' present and their hopes for the future. The present crisis reforms their memory of the past. The God who once delivered will deliver again.

The reading of the Bible in liberation theology is communitarian. It is not essentially a matter of individual piety. The Bible is matched with the community's life of sorrow and joy. The reading begins with experience (which for the majority of third world Christians is an experience of poverty), and in actual practice, before the reading of the Bible, questions from life are formulated by discussing actual situations. The way may be opened by the telling of a significant story or by showing a picture; the goal is to lead participants into a conversation that then results in the expression of the problem by the participants themselves. Then, a biblical text is chosen and applied to the experience. The readers understand the biblical text as addressed essentially to them, not to ancient readers. This does away with the distance between the ancient text and the reader.

One liberation reading practice identifies biblical people, actions, and events more or less directly with those of the present time. The assumption is that the Christian community can be related to its political context in precisely the same way that Jesus was related to his political context. Roman power is modern imperialism; the Sadducees are the dependent bourgeoisie; the Zealots are the revolutionaries. The Gospel comes to life when it is read from the perspective of the circumstances in the readers' lives.

Critical attention to the text, however, does not make it less applicable to the lives of the people. The reading practice may give attention to historical relationships rather than to terms. Instead of a direct "correspondence of terms" there is a "correspondence of relationships." In order to sort out the relationships, historical study is used, but the agenda is not simply to research and represent the past. The agenda is to read the Scriptures so as to be faithful to the way the texts responded to the needs of the communities for whom they were composed. Instead of a simplistic equation of the political engagement of Jesus and the political engagement of Christians, the political engagement of Jesus vis-à-vis the historical social context at that time is seen as related to the political engagement of Christians vis-à-vis the current social context.

The immediate, free, subjective, and emancipatory character of Bible reading in liberation theology can be illustrated from Ernesto Cardinal's transcripts of Bible study groups in Nicaragua.[16] Instead of a sermon, there would be a dialogue between Ernesto and the *campesinos* who attended the service. The following comments of a young Nicaraguan (reflecting the situation in Nicaragua before the Sadinista revolution in 1979) links the oppressive conditions in twentieth century Central America with the colonial oppression of first century Judea. The extract has Laureano presenting a reading of the passage about tribute money:

> It isn't that the money belonged to the emperor; the money belonged to the people, but Jesus tells them to notice the coin, so that they can see what imperialism is: a coin with a face of a man there. He wanted them to see that from the time when the emperor puts his name and face on a coin he's making himself boss of everything in the country, of everybody, of the money that belongs to everybody. And Jesus is showing them that Caesar's a complete dictator because he's putting his portrait on the coin and taking for himself what belongs to the people. He's telling them that he's grabbing the money, because he's pictured there as owner and lord of everything; then he wants to make himself owner even of the people, because he was on the money with which the people were buying. Let's say that it's like this now in Nicaragua, with Somoza, because Somoza is on the money, and we're all used to seeing him as the owner of Nicaragua; that's the way it was at the time. I believe he wants to tell them that all things belong to God, but that the emperor wants to make himself owner of everything when he makes himself owner of people's money.[17]

Students of liberation theology find the heart of liberation exegesis to be "the renewal of old traditions in the light of new situations." This reading practice "has nothing to do with the desire to manipulate the text. It has to do with a willingness on the part of the interpreter to allow himself or herself to be manipulated by the text, to allow the Sitz-im-Leben of the reader to be criticized and judged by the Word of God. It is a form of exegesis that is willing to make the reader vulnerable to the scriptural content. . . ."[18]

Conclusion: Varieties of Readings and the Word of God

How may these different ways of reading be coordinated? Contemporary readers who desire to maintain a healthy religious life and a sane and productive intellectual existence will not elevate one way so as to eliminate other ways of reading. They are able to engage all of the different ways of reading, and in different contexts to privilege particular reading styles. But other styles remain on the horizon, influencing the reading of the moment and capable of becoming the focus. In the academy, the historical-critical and literary approaches may be emphasized. In the church, however, readers may begin with concern for the Bible's contribution to the life of believers, the Bible as revelation and word of God. Modern readers will not want to engage in an uncritical credulous reading, however. They will move to critical approaches, therefore, to clarify and support their understanding of the message of the Bible as word of God (as historical-critical approaches assist feminist and liberation readings). Literary approaches may be followed to enable readers to appreciate the way the way that the language of the Bible functions as art, and the Bible becomes meaningful as an aesthetic object. However, creative literary approaches may also assist in the wedding of the religious message and the historical and sociological circumstances of origin.

The different ways of reading illuminate different functions of the Bible and different needs of readers. We read as individuals and in groups. We read for intellectual and spiritual sustenance and guidance. We read for relationship and fellowship with God. We read so that our pilgrimage may be illuminated and inspired by the experience of the word of God that has been stamped onto the words of Scripture, so that the "record of God's revelation" of God's self may become revelation for us in our day.[19]

Notes

[1] See James L. Kugel, *The Bible as It Was* (Cambridge MA and London: Harvard University Press, 1997), 17-23 for a detailed discussion of these four characteristics of reading the Hebrew Bible as oracle. John Barton uses the terms "profound," "universally relevant," "internally consistent," and "mysterious" to describe the assumptions directing reading as the New Testament canon was formed (John Barton, *Holy Writings, Sacred Text: The Canon in Early Christianity* [Louisville: Westminster John Knox, 1997]).

[2] John Cassian, *The Conferences* (New York: Paulist Press, 1997), 510.

[3] Raymond E. Brown and Sandra M. Schneiders, "Hermeneutics," *The New Jerome Biblical Commentary* (Englewood Cliffs NJ: Prentice Hall, 1990), 1157.

[4] Augustine, *On Christian Doctrine* 3.10.14.

[5] Ibid., 2.6.7-8.

[6] Roland Barthes, "The Struggle with the Angel: Textual Analysis of Genesis 32:23-33," *Structural Analysis and Biblical Exegesis*, ed. R. Barthes, F. Bovon, et al. (Pittsburg: Pickwick Press, 1974), 21-33.

[7] David Rhoads, Joanna Dewey, and Donald Michie, *Mark as Story: An Introduction to the Narrative of a Gospel*, 2d ed. (Minneapolis: Fortress Press, 1999), 61-62.

[8] Hans Dieter Betz, *Galatians: A Commentary on Paul's Letter to the Churches in Galatia*, Hermenia (Philadelphia: Fortress, 1979).

[9] Jeffrey Rogers, "And a Little Child Shall Lead Them," sermon, First Baptist Church, Greenville SC, 8 July 2001.

[10] See David J. A. Clines, "A World Established on Water (Psalm 24): Reader-response, Deconstruction and Bespoke Interpretation," *The New Literary Criticism and the Hebrew Bible*, ed. J. Cheryl Exum and David J. A. Clines (Sheffield: Sheffield Academic Press, 1993), 79-90.

[11] For a treatment of the different ways feminists read Genesis 2–3, see Danna Nolan Fewell, "Reading the Bible Ideologically: Feminist Criticism," *To Each Its Own Meaning: An Introduction to Biblical Criticism and Their Application*, 2d ed. (Louisville: Westminster/John Knox Press, 1999), 268-82.

[12] See Phyllis Bird, "Genesis 1–3 as a Source for a Contemporary Theology of Sexuality," *Ex Auditu* (1987): 31-44.

[13] First argued by Phyllis Trible in "Depatriarchalizing in Biblical Interpretation," *Journal of the American Academy of Religion* 41 (1973): 30-48.

[14] J. Cheryl Exum, "'You Shall Let Every Daughter Live': A Study of Exodus 1:8–2:10," *Semeia* 28 (1983): 63-82.

[15] Janice Capel Anderson, "Matthew: Gender and Reading," *Semeia* 28 (1983): 21.

[16] These were published in English under the title *Love in Practice: The Gospel in Solentiname*, 4 vols. (Mary Knoll NY: Obis Books, 1977–1984).

[17] E. Cardenal, *Love in Practice: The Gospel in Solentiname*, vol. 3, p. 284; cited in Christopher Rowland and Mark Corner, *Liberating Exegesis: The Challenge of Liberation Theology to Biblical Studies* (Louisville: Westminster/John Knox, 1989), 17.

[18] Rowland and Corner, 69.

[19] Readers familiar wtih my writings will note the significance accorded to literary approaches in the present work compared with that in *Opening the Bible: A Guide to Understanding the Scriptures* (Nashville: Broadman Press, 1967), a volume that introduced readers to the values of the historical-critical approach. This final chapter on "Varieties of Readings: Credulous, Critical, and Creative Approaches" appears in a shorter revised form in the *New Interpreters Study Bible: New Revised Standard Version With the Apocrypha* (Nashville: Abingdon Press, 2003), Walter J. Harrelson, editor.

children, adults who read at or below the fourth-grade level, and those for whom English is a second language.

The New International Readers Version and an edition of the New International Version published in Britain (1995) are language-inclusive versions. These editions did not replace masculine references to God with neutral or feminine language, but they did use gender-inclusive language where the translators decided that the biblical writers did not intend their language to exclude either gender. Success of these translations led the president of the International Bible Society to promise the production of an inclusive-language New International Version in North America. This plan was originally canceled when leaders of large rigid evangelical and fundamentalist groups expressed their displeasure. The basis for displeasure was their belief that the subordination of women to men is a divinely-ordained state of affairs and the threat that a gender-inclusive translation would be to this belief. One leader said that the proposed inclusive-language version was part of a "feminist effort to re-engineer society and abandon God's parameters for the home and for the church."[7] With the forceful expressions of disagreement, the International Bible Society decided to drop plans for an inclusive language edition of the New International Version in the United States, to revise the New International Readers Version so that it would contain *exclusive* language, and to ask its British publisher (Hodder & Stoughton) to withdraw its already-published inclusive-language New International Version.

By the spring of 2002, the International Bible Society recognized the short-sightedness of its decision to drop plans for an American inclusive language edition. The New Testament portion of Today's New International Version was published and the majority of the instances of the generic use of masculine nouns and pronouns were removed. The preface to the TNIV New Testament declares without apology:

> While a basic core of the English language remains relatively stable, many diverse and complex cultural forces continue to bring about subtle changes in the meanings and/or connotations of even old, well-established words and phrases. Among the more programmatic changes in the TNIV is the removal of nearly all vocative "O"s and the elimination of most instances of the generic use of masculine nouns and pronouns. Relative to the second of these, the so-called singular "they/their/them," which has been gaining acceptance among careful writers and which actually has a venerable place in English idiom, has been employed to fill in the vocabulary gap in generic nouns and pronouns referring to human beings. Where an individual emphasis is deemed to be present, "anyone" or "everyone" is generally used as the antecedent of such pronouns.

Conservative evangelical opposition continued, and at its 2002 meeting, the messengers to the Southern Baptist Convention adopted a resolution expressing "profound disappointment" in the International Bible Society and in Zondervan Press for "this inaccurate translation."

The New Revised Standard Version and The Revised English Bible. The New Revised Standard Version and the Revised English Bible were published in 1989. Both of these translations are based on the most acceptable scholarly versions of ancient texts, and both are designed for use in public worship and well as for use in serious Bible study. Both are also designed to update and clarify the language of their predecessors and they may be compared with one another in this regard.

The Revised English Bible is a thorough revision of the New English Bible and deserves praise for its readability. It must be considered a cautiously-framed functional-equivalence translation, attempting to use ordinary English rather than "theological" terminology. The New Revised Standard Version is a somewhat free verbal-equivalence translation. The preface "To the Reader" advises:

> This new version seeks to preserve all that is best in the English Bible as it has been known and used through the years. It is intended for use in public reading and congregational worship, as well as in private study, instruction, and meditation. We have resisted the temptation to introduce terms and phrases that merely reflect current moods, and have tried to put the message of the Scriptures in simple, enduring words and expressions that are worthy to stand in the great tradition of the King James Bible and its predecessors.

Earlier in the preface the translation is spoken of as "essentially a literal translation" and "as literal as possible, as free as necessary."

The translators of the New Revised Standard Version did not give attention to references to the "Jews" in the New Testament as part of their conscious agenda. The Revised Standard Version is seen by David G. Burke, a representative of the American Bible Society, as being one of the least sensitive translations in regard to the treatment of references to "the Jews" and he indicates that the New Revised Standard Version makes only slight adjustments. The same thing may be said of the Revised English Bible. There seem to be advances in some verses while other verses show a lack of sensitivity. In terms of inclusive language, both translations consciously seek to avoid male-oriented language and move toward gender-inclusive language. They succeed at times and fail at times. Carol R. Fontaine compares the two translations in terms of their use of inclusive language and gives her overall evaluation of the two translations: